Pelican Books
Fift...

G. F. Hudson is in charge of Far Eastern
Studies at St Antony's College, Oxford. He has
made a special study of the effect of Communism
in Eastern Europe and in the Far and Middle
East.

His other publications include *Europe and
China*, *The Far East in World Politics*, *Turkey, Greece
and the Eastern Mediterranean*, *British and American
Policies in the Far East since 1900*, *The Fanatic and
the Sane*, *The Hard and Bitter Peace*.

G. F. Hudson

Fifty Years
of Communism

Theory and Practice 1917–1967

Penguin Books

Penguin Books Ltd, Harmondsworth,
Middlesex, England
Penguin Books Inc., 7110 Ambassador Road,
Baltimore, Maryland 21207, U.S.A.
Penguin Books Australia Ltd, Ringwood,
Victoria, Australia

First published by C. A. Watts & Co. 1968
Published in Pelican Books 1971
Reprinted 1972
Copyright © G. F. Hudson, 1968

Made and printed in Great Britain
by Richard Clay (The Chaucer Press) Ltd,
Bungay, Suffolk
Set in Linotype Baskerville

Contents

Preface

At the time when the Communists came to power in China someone remarked that commentators on the event could be divided into those who knew something about China, but nothing about Communism, and those who knew something about Communism, but nothing about China. It is indeed extremely difficult for anyone to combine the kind of knowledge of Communism which comes from a study of its ideology and mental processes with an expertise on particular countries which are affected by the world Communist movement. Yet the attempt must be made, for if it is not, interpretations of current international affairs will either fail in understanding of one of the main political ideas of our time or else be confined to analyses of abstract doctrine without taking account of the local historical settings in which the doctrine wins its followers.

This book aims at a review of the development of Communism, both in theory and in practice, since the Bolshevik capture of power in Russia in 1917, with a preliminary account of the origins of Marxism and its introduction into Russia from its homeland in Western Europe. The Russian Communists modified Marxism and the Chinese Communists have modified it still more. Today a large part of mankind lives under governments which acknowledge Marx as their ideological ancestor, but Marxism has assumed strange shapes which would evoke his astonishment, and often his indignation, if he could return to this world to view the effects of his life's work.

In the writing of this book I have had the benefit of many discussions of its themes with colleagues in the

PREFACE

Centres of Soviet and Far Eastern Studies in St Antony's College. I wish also to express my gratitude to Dr Werner Klatt for much information and enlightenment about both Soviet and Chinese affairs and to Mr Roderick MacFarquhar, Editor of *China Quarterly*, for many stimulating initiatives in the study of Chinese Communism.

G. F. H.

1. Jacobin and Communist

In the seventeenth and eighteenth centuries France provided the continent of Europe with its model of monarchical power and courtly elegance; in the nineteenth she provided the model of popular revolution. The myth of the French Revolution was the inspiration of all those who in the years between the end of the Napoleonic Empire in 1815 and the revolutionary upheavals of 1848 sought to bring about radical changes in the established political and social order. Paris in those years, even though it was the seat of the restored Bourbons and then of the 'bourgeois monarchy' of Louis Philippe, remained the Mecca of all the revolutionaries of Europe, for it was the city which possessed within itself the tradition of the Great Revolution and continued to be the hotbed of radical political thought.

It is at first sight something of a paradox that a historical period which had violently broken with the traditional values and institutions of its society should have itself created so powerful a tradition. But so it was; for those to whom the brief rule of the French revolutionary democracy was not a dire example of what to avoid it was the pattern of success to be regained. Europe might have fallen back under the domination of royal autocracies or narrow oligarchies, but what had been done could be done again and the sovereignty of the people once more established in all its power and glory. The Bastille could again be captured; there could be another Robespierre and another Marat. Those who in the 1840s were moved by the ideal of democracy – an ideal which in the actual political condition of Europe was then still revolutionary – could not do otherwise than look back to the days of the First Republic for their paragons and their precedents. Yet the world had changed since the knife of the guillotine had descended on the neck of Robespierre, and the social situation in France on the eve of the Revolution of 1848 was profoundly different from what it had been in the time of the Jacobins. The half century which began with the Directory had seen the phenomenal growth of *la grande industrie*, the expansion of that large-scale capitalist economy which in 1789 had been in its earliest infancy. And with the growth of capitalist industry had grown also its complement, the class of wage-earning industrial workers. In the time of the Jacobins the working people of Paris, of whose interests they made themselves the champions, were predominantly self-employed artisans or apprentices and assistants who hoped themselves to become independent craftsmen. By 1848 they were in their great majority wage-workers. This fact was to give the Revolution of 1848 a fundamentally different character from that of 1789. The forces of the Commune of Paris which in June 1793 gave the Jacobins their victory over the Gironde represented a *petite bourgeoisie* which, however poverty-stricken, was still attached to the principle of private ownership of the means of production; the Parisian workers who in June of 1848 fought against the army of Cavaignac were a propertyless proletariat for whom that principle no longer had the same value.

Already in the time of the First Republic a few of the most extreme Jacobins had arrived at the belief that political democracy would be insufficient to ensure the equality at which they aimed unless there were to be also an ownership of, or at least a decisive control over, the means of production by the state. Babeuf and his associates developed a proto-socialist doctrine after the overthrow of the Jacobin dictatorship; in contrast to the general trend towards social reaction under the Directory they sought political salvation in courses even more extreme than those of Robespierre and Marat, and hoped to find a new basis for power in the poorest elements of the population. They formed a small conspiratorial group, and, as ex-Jacobins, they conceived of popular power, not as an authority to be exercised through a freely elected parliamentary assembly of the whole people, but as what Professor Talmon has called 'totalitarian democracy', that is to say, as a dictatorship exercised by an enlightened and dedicated elite on behalf of the masses, who were regarded as too ignorant and unorganized and too preoccupied with time-consuming manual labour to be able to take part effectively in politics. The Babeuvists never succeeded in bringing about an insurrection; their plotting was detected by the police of the Directory and their leaders were arrested and executed. They nevertheless left behind them a revolutionary tradition which supplemented that of the Jacobins; Buonarroti, who was a follower of Babeuf, and who became the prototype of the 'professional revolutionary', lived to be the teacher of Blanqui, who was, in the words of George Lichtheim, 'the last Jacobin and the first Communist'.[1]

The transition from the democratic doctrine of the original French Revolution to the collectivism of nineteenth-century radical thought – which came to be known as socialism or communism, both terms being at one time used more or less as synonyms – was brought about through the writings of a group of social theorists among whom Fourier and Saint-Simon were the most influential. These were the thinkers on whom historians under the influence of Marxist polemics have been too willing to pin the label of 'Utopian' in contrast to the 'scientific' socialism of Marx and Engels. But their visions of the future were not so much more Utopian than those of Marx and, as Joll has pointed out in his study of anarchism, Saint-Simon 'was the first thinker to analyse historical change in terms of the struggle between social and

1. George Lichtheim, *Marxism*, p. 89 n.

economic classes'.[2] What differentiates these pioneers from Marx and his followers is the absence of the influence of Hegel which provided the Marxists with their all-embracing philosophy of history. They were also, in contrast to Marx and Engels, detached from actual politics, but this was almost a necessity of their time, for in the period of the Restoration in France there was hardly any scope for radical political agitation; a mild bourgeois liberalism marked the limit of serious dissent. It was only later that socialist speculations nurtured in the realm of philosophy and literature began to be linked with the grievances and aspirations of the ever-growing industrial proletariat, and the process by which socialism thus became a political force must be attributed, in the first place, not to Marx and his Communist League, but to the French conspiratorial groups led by Blanqui and others, notably the Société des Saisons,[3] which were in close contact with the working class of Paris. The League of Communists was a German branch of the French movement; it drew its inspiration from France, but just because German industry in the 1840s was far behind the French in its development, and the German industrial proletariat correspondingly much smaller, the German version of the faith tended to be more extreme and doctrinaire than the French. The choice of the name 'communist' was an indication of this; it had come to have a slightly sharper and more uncompromising connotation than the word 'socialist', which was preferred by the French. Engels later explained that the *Communist Manifesto* was so called because 'whatever portion of the working class had become convinced of the insufficiency of mere political revolutions and had proclaimed the necessity for a total social change called itself communist', whereas the word 'socialist' was associated with the Utopians and with 'the most multifarious social quacks, who by all manner of tinkering professed to redress,

2. James Joll, *The Anarchists*, p. 53.
3. Lichtheim, op. cit., p. 123 n.

without any danger to capital and profit, all sorts of social grievances'.

In Marx himself it is possible to trace two dominant formative influences; that of the Hegelian philosophy, which he underwent during his higher education in Germany, and that of the French Jacobin-Babeuvist revolutionary tradition, with which he came into direct contact when he went to France in 1843. Hegel came first, and it was his philosophy that provided the ultimate intellectual foundation of Marxism. The outstanding achievement of Hegel was a synthesis which reconciled the principle of a transcendental unity of being with that of a progressive movement of human history conceived as a gradual unfolding, through conflicts of opposites, of man's knowledge and comprehension of the cosmos. As formulated by Hegel himself in his later years, this was a highly spiritual, and even mystical, philosophy, and it could be used as a support of the established social and political order through his willingness to regard the Prussian state of the early nineteenth century as the climax of human endeavour. But it was not difficult for his followers to discard the spiritual and transcendental side of Hegel's philosophy and concentrate on his theory of historical progress, in which human reason was destined to conquer, but only through contradiction and struggle. For students of Hegelianism who could not agree that contemporary Prussia was the last word in human evolution it followed that the next forward movement of mankind was to be expected from those who were least involved in support of the existing order of things, and from this belief it was only a short step to the affirmation that the future lay with the industrial proletariat, the new class which had nothing to lose but its chains, but had a world to win.

Marx, however, did not definitely reach this conclusion until he had left Germany for Paris in 1843 after the Prussian censorship had forced him out of his post as editor of the *Rheinische Zeitung*. His activity as a

Rhineland journalist had been enough to infuriate Prussian officialdom, which found that 'his ultra-democratic opinions are in utter contradiction to the principles of the Prussian state', but he was not then regarded as a communist, nor had he yet been exposed directly to the ferment of French radical thought, of which only a weak and distant influence had penetrated into Germany. It was in Paris that he came into immediate contact with the leading exponents of contemporary socialist thought, and also with a population of workers among whom there were still living people who could remember Robespierre. It was in this environment that he wrote for the *Deutsch-Französische Jahrbücher* – published in France to evade the Prussian censorship – his *Introduction to a Critique of the Hegelian Philosophy of Law*, wherein his commitment to the cause of proletarian socialist revolution is for the first time clearly affirmed.

The basic Marxist doctrine was thus formulated, but it still remained far removed from that world of contemporary economic development with which in theory it was so vitally concerned. The element of empirical observation and fact finding was added by Engels, whose lifelong friendship with Marx dated from 1843, when they collaborated in a polemical work attacking the German literary and philosophical coterie headed by Bruno Bauer. Engels came from a social milieu significantly different from that in which Marx had been brought up. The son of a lawyer and grandson of a rabbi, Marx belonged to the professional middle class, but not to the commercial bourgeoisie; Engels, on the other hand, was born into a prosperous business family and in spite of a personal preference for intellectual pursuits took part in the manning of the family firm. Engels was at one time a Hegelian and knew enough of this philosophy to understand what Marx was talking about, but his own main interest was in the economic field and in the actual contemporary social effects of the system of capitalist industry in which he was himself willy-nilly an operator. In 1845 he published in Germany a book entitled *The Condition of the Working Class in England in 1844*, a work which not only added an element of empirical study to the general philosophical view which Marx and Engels had come to share, but also added the influence of a third country, England, to the contributions already made to Marxism by Germany and France. Engels had lived for two years in England in an English branch of the family business, and had thus acquired a direct acquaintance, not only with the workings of the capitalist system as such, but also with its performance in the country where it was at that time most highly developed. England was still the 'workshop of the world', the most urbanized and industrialized of all European nations, and therefore the country which afforded the best field for the study of industrial capitalism in practice. It was also the country in which the new theoretical science of economics had been carried furthest. Yet there was a paradox in the English example which is historically significant because it anticipates a situation which has kept on cropping up in Marxist theory down to the present day. It was undoubtedly implicit in the Marxist conception of the historical mission of the proletariat as a class produced by capitalism, but destined by the dialectic of history to be its destroyer, that the revolutionary explosion should come first in the country where capitalist industry was most highly developed and the proletariat most numerous. By this logic England should be the country with the greatest socialist revolutionary potential. But this was not in fact so; in spite of the sufferings of the English working class during the 'Hungry Forties' and its exclusion from the franchise until 1867, it proved strangely unresponsive to appeals for violent action; in the year 1848 revolution flamed in Paris, Vienna and Berlin, but in London nothing happened. It had been the same in 1789–94, when the upheaval in France had found sympathizers beyond the Channel, but no serious imitation. Failure then to follow the French lead could be attri-

buted in Central and Eastern Europe to the backwardness of the old-fashioned 'feudal' agrarian societies, but
this explanation could not apply to England, where the
economic evolution of the bourgeoisie had already gone
further than in France. Unless the cause were to be
sought in some innate national characteristics – which
themselves would be inexplicable apart from the history
of national formations in Europe – it had to be recognized that there had been in England a degree of political
compromise and adjustment which reduced the prob-
ability of a violent revolutionary outcome of social tensions. In the view of European history adopted by Marx
and Engels, England had already had her bourgeois revolution in the seventeenth century; the upheaval of the
1640s had like the French Revolution a hundred and
fifty years later put an end to royal autocracy, had
formally executed a king and had prepared the way for
parliamentary power. But the political system of England in the eighteenth century was not a bourgeois democracy, and can hardly be called bourgeois at all. The
eighteenth century was the golden age of the English
landed aristocracy. What made it tolerable for the rising
commercial class – as the *ancien régime* in France was
not – was a political structure which drew the most
important line of division between peers and commoners,
and not, as was normal in continental Europe, between
nobles and burghers. The peers had their hereditary
seats in the House of Lords, while the gentry of the
counties were, with the boroughs, represented in the
House of Commons, and this arrangement produced a
degree of class fusion below the peerage which gave the
political order a relatively stable social base. In spite of
Wilkes and an emerging social radicalism it stood firm
against the waves of shock emanating from the French
Revolution, and in 1832, without any violence greater
than that of local riots, reformed the parliamentary franchise to allow for representation of the new industrial
bourgeoisie, which had had to fight its way as much

against the older entrenched financial and commercial interests as against the power of the landlords. The new industrial working class still remained without political representation, but it was confronted with a formidable grouping of classes which already enjoyed full political rights, and although there were advocates of 'physical force' among the Chartists, English politics had developed for so long through a series of non-violent adjustments to changing conditions that it had become natural to expect similar adjustments of the same kind in future. Thus, although England was the country which had gone furthest in the development of industrial capitalism, and should have been in Marxist theory the nearest to the historically predestined proletarian revolution, it was in fact singularly infertile ground for the seeds of revolutionary socialist propaganda.

It was in France rather than England that the growing industrial proletariat had revolutionary inclinations, and this was the outcome of a situation in which the rule of the Jacobins was a matter of recent memory and the existing regime, that of the Orleanist monarchy, was itself the product of a revolutionary uprising in 1830. The reign of Louis Philippe was acceptable neither to the Bourbon legitimists whom it had supplanted nor to those who remained in the tradition of the Great Revolution and would be satisfied with nothing less than a democratic republic. The working class of Paris tended to regard the democratic republic as a minimum requirement; scourged by unemployment after the trade recession of 1847, it claimed the 'right to work' and demanded that the government of the state should assume the responsibility of providing employment for workers not needed in private industry, a demand which, even though not accompanied by advocacy of public ownership of all means of production, involved a formidable challenge to the existing economic system. When in February 1848 the republican revolution overthrew the Orleanist monarchy the new government sought to placate the

Parisian proletariat by setting up the 'National Workshops' to provide employment, but with disastrous results, for no plans had been made for profitable production in new enterprises and the workshops became an intolerable burden on the financial resources of the state as destitute workmen flocked to Paris from all over France to partake in the benefits of the new public bounty. The government's attempt to restrict the scheme provoked in June an armed insurrection, which was crushed only by hard fighting and the use of artillery to overcome the workers manning barricades in the streets of Paris. This was the nearest thing to a proletarian revolution that happened in Europe in 1848. It was a sign of the times and it made a deep impression on contemporary observers. But it was, after all, a complete failure; it lasted only for four days and its main effect was to unite all propertied classes in opposition to the aspirations of the propertyless wage-earners. The Parisian proletariat had received no support from the non-proletarian sections of the population; neither the *haute bourgeoisie* nor the *petite bourgeoisie* nor the peasants, the bulk of whom were since the Great Revolution proprietors of the land they tilled, were prepared to pay taxes to maintain the National Workshops, and even less to endorse projects for a general expropriation of private property. The French proletariat of 1848 might be more militant than the English, but it proved no more capable of taking over the power of the state.

Yet it was neither to England nor to France that Marx and Engels looked primarily at the beginning of the year for the revolution of their dreams; it was to their own country – to Germany. In spite of the fact that modern industry was so much less developed there than in England or France, and the wage-earning working class correspondingly smaller, Marx and Engels entertained extravagant hopes of success for their League of Communists in the confusion that they expected to follow the collapse of the absolute monarchies in Prussia and

Austria. In the words of the *Communist Manifesto*, which they wrote at the end of 1847: [4]

The Communists turn their attention chiefly to Germany because that country is on the eve of a bourgeois revolution that is bound to be carried out under more advanced conditions of European civilization and with a much more developed proletariat than that of England in the seventeenth and of France in the eighteenth century, and because the bourgeois revolution in Germany will be but the prelude to an immediately following proletarian revolution.

The expectation in this passage is clearly that the chances of a proletarian revolution in Germany are greater because the monarchies there have remained autocratic and are not cushioned against the shocks of popular upheaval by parliaments as in France or England; there is a recognition that, contrary to the theoretical requirement that socialist revolution is nearest in the most highly developed industrial country, a society in which the bourgeoisie has already consolidated its characteristic parliamentary institutions is likely to offer a stronger resistance to a seizure of political power by the proletariat than one in which a traditional feudal-monarchical order has remained intact and is then suddenly overthrown. Under a system of royal autocracy everyone is accustomed to receive orders from above and there is no large number of persons with the habit of independent political activity of a non-conspiratorial kind, so that, if and when the royal authority collapses, it is extremely difficult for a stable parliamentary republican regime to be at once established in its place. The best opportunity for the adherents of a really radical revolutionary faith lies in the interval between the downfall of an *ancien régime* and the consolidation of a new bourgeois order. Thus in the original French Revolution

4. The *Communist Manifesto* was drawn up in German and sent to the printer a few weeks before the Paris insurrection of 24 February 1848.

the Jacobins were able to capture power in the confusion and vacuum of authority which followed the collapse of the Bourbon monarchy; more than a century later the Russian Bolsheviks captured power in the period of 'passive anarchy' which followed the extinction of the Tsardom. Marx and Engels, with the example of the French Revolution behind them, hoped for a similar opportunity in the anticipated German Revolution of 1848. Their hopes, however, were not destined to be fulfilled. Nobody can say what might have happened if the monarchies in Berlin and Vienna had been swept away and politicians of the Girondin type had tried to govern Germany after a complete dissolution of the previous political order. But the monarchies were not swept away; they remained, with powerful armies loyal to them, and before long they recovered control of their capitals where popular insurgency had had a brief hour of triumph. What the bourgeois revolution gained was a parliament in Prussia, but this parliament controlled neither the political executive nor the army, and within two decades it had bowed the knee to Bismarck when Prussia under his leadership carried out that national unification of Germany which the liberals of 1848 had been unable to accomplish. The League of Communists took an active part in helping forward whatever bourgeois revolution there was in Germany, but as this revolution was never completed, there could be no question of a proletarian revolution 'immediately following'.

Marx lived for thirty-four years after the disappointment of his hopes in 1848 and he never saw a successful communist revolution in his lifetime. But a little over three decades after his death a situation similar to that which he had expected in Germany in 1848 actually did occur in Russia, and Lenin, as a follower of Marx, took advantage of it. In March 1917 the Russian Tsardom was brought to an end, and during the next eight months nobody was able to organize a stable government in Russia. In November Lenin seized power.

2. Social Democracy and the Non-revolution

The failure of a political enterprise intended to bring about a fundamental change in the order of society can have one of three different effects on a man who has undertaken it. He may go on trying to do the same thing in the same way, always hoping that he will have better luck next time. Or he may come to the conclusion that his whole effort is futile and that he may as well accept the established order of things. Or he may continue to adhere to his faith, but recognize that the difficulties are greater than he had previously supposed and that he must adopt a more gradual method of approach to a goal which has receded into the far distance.

It was the third of these courses that Marx and Engels took after the year 1850, and in consequence there is a great difference between the Marxism of the years before that date and the later Marxism which was to become the creed of the Social Democratic Party of Germany. What is called Leninism, the outlook characteristic of all modern Communists, at any rate before the Twentieth Congress of the Soviet Communist Party in 1956, is essentially a reversion to the older Marxism, the doctrine of the *Communist Manifesto* of 1848, as against that of the Introduction written by Engels in 1895 to the work of Marx *The Class Struggles in France* written in 1850. These reflections by Engels towards the close of the nineteenth century were in effect a repudiation of the bold words of the *Communist Manifesto* that the Communists 'openly declare that their ends can be attained only by the forcible overthrow of all existing social institutions'. By 1895 Engels had come to the conclusion that the forcible seizure of power in a modern European state was not a practical proposition, and that 'the mode of struggle of 1848 is today obsolete from every point of view'. On the other hand, as he saw it, a new road to socialism had opened up for the working class through the use of universal suffrage as a means of non-violent political change. Engels did not even in 1895 deny the right of the workers to use force, and he still considered that it might in some circumstances be unavoidable, to meet attacks on rights already gained by the workers, but he had come to believe that a democratic parliamentary constitution afforded sufficient scope for an advance towards the socialist goal. The very change of name from 'communist' to 'socialist' or 'social democrat' was significant of the transition from the heroic all-or-nothing revolutionary conception of the *Communist Manifesto* to a more modest, gradual and peaceful form of political action.

In 1850, when Marx still hoped for a new wave of revolutionary disturbance in Germany, he gave advice in his *Address to the Communist League* on the methods to be used in preparing and carrying out a proletarian *coup de force*. In the struggle against the old feudal-monarchical order the workers must make common cause with the bourgeois democrats, but they must build up and preserve their own independent organization, so that when victory over the common enemy has been obtained, they may be ready for the struggle against their former political allies. 'While the democratic petty bourgeoisie,' he declares, 'would like to bring the revolution to a close as soon as their demands are more or less complied with, it is in our interest and our taste to make the revolution permanent, to keep it going until all the ruling and possessing classes are deprived of power.' For this purpose the Communists 'must act in such a manner that the revolutionary excitement does not subside immediately after the victory' over the reactionary enemy, and alongside the new official government they must set up a revolutionary workers' government in the form of local committees and councils so that the new bourgeois regime finds itself from the outset 'under the supervision and threats of authorities behind whom stands the entire mass of the working class'. To give strength to these proletarian 'authorities' and frustrate the bourgeois democrats in their endeavour to stop the revolution from going further

... it is necessary to organize and arm the proletariat. The arming of the whole proletariat with rifles, guns and ammunition must be carried out at once; we must prevent the revival of the old bourgeois militia which has always been directed against the workers. Where the latter measure cannot be carried out, the workers must try to organize themselves into an independent guard, with their own chiefs and general staff, and obey orders, not of the government, but only of the revolutionary authorities set up by the workers.... Under no pretext must they give up their arms and equipment, and any attempt at disarmament must be forcibly resisted.

There is no need to emphasize the similarity of the course here recommended to what actually happened in Russia in 1917, when the soviets of workers' and soldiers' delegates were set up as rival authorities at the side of the Provisional Government after the revolution which overthrew the Tsardom in March of that year. In Germany in 1850, however, nothing of the kind took place. Moreover, in advocating such tactics Marx was arguing from general theoretical considerations and from historical precedents; he was himself a man of the pen and not of the sword, and he had no direct experience either of revolutionary warfare or of any sort of military service. Engels on the other hand had served for a year in a regiment of the Prussian army, so that he had some knowledge of military affairs, and in 1849 he became adjutant of a volunteer corps raised to take part in the short-lived republican insurrection in Baden. He thus had a keener appreciation than Marx of what was actually involved in an attempt to capture the power of the state by force, and there was sound sense in what he had to say on the subject in 1895:

Let us have no illusions about it; a real victory of an insurrection over the military in street fighting, a victory as between two armies, is one of the rarest exceptions. But the insurgents also counted on it just as rarely. For them it was solely a question of making the troops yield to moral influences.... If they succeed in this, then the troops fail to act, or the commanding officers lose their heads, and the insurrection wins. If they do not succeed, then, even when the military are outnumbered, their better equipment and training, their discipline and unity of command make themselves felt. No wonder then that even barricade struggles conducted with the greatest heroism, as in Paris in June 1848, in Vienna in October 1848 and in Dresden in May 1849, ended in defeat when the leaders of the counter-revolutionary attack acted from a purely military standpoint and their soldiers remained reliable.

Since 1849, according to Engels, technological factors had increased the capacity of organized military forces, as long as they remained loyal to the established government, to crush popular insurrections.

Paris and Berlin have since 1849 grown less than fourfold, but their garrisons have grown more than that. By means of railways the garrisons can be doubled in twenty-four hours and in forty-eight hours they can be increased to big armies. The armies of the vastly increased numbers of troops have also become incomparably more effective. In 1848 the smooth-bore percussion muzzle-loader; today the small-calibre magazine breech-loading rifle, which shoots four times as far, ten times as accurately and ten times as fast as the former. In 1848 the relatively ineffective roundshot and grapeshot of the artillery; today the percussion shells, one of which is sufficient to demolish the best barricade.

Engels is thus at pains to pour cold water on the ardour of any young proletarian revolutionaries who might still dream in 1895 of storming the Bastilles of capitalism in the capital cities of Europe. But this did not mean that they must abandon the struggle and make their submission to the bourgeois social order. There was another way forward. The German Social Democratic Party had shown the workers of all countries how to make use of universal suffrage. The Social Democratic vote had increased steadily until it could count more than a quarter of all votes cast in elections for the Reichstag. Engels claimed that the rise of the vote had 'increased in equal measure the workers' certainty of victory and the dismay of their opponents' and in consequence 'the bourgeoisie and the government came to be much more afraid of the legal than of the illegal action of the workers' party, of the results of elections than of those of rebellions'.

Universal suffrage had had little appeal for Marxists in earlier days. The state, with its bureaucracy, its police and its armed forces, had seemed to them to be too firmly in the hands of the ruling classes, whether aristocratic or bourgeois, for the workers to be able to capture it by winning elections, even if they could obtain the majority of seats in a parliament; only by a *coup de force* which would transfer the state power to an insurgent proletariat could an expropriation of the propertied classes be brought about. The enfranchisement of the masses had been traditionally regarded by socialists as a *duperie*, and the experience of the Second Republic, when it brought power to Louis Napoleon, confirmed these feelings of mistrust for it as a means for attaining ultimate social objectives. It was indeed a demand in which the workers could join with bourgeois democrats against oligarchies based on limited franchises, but its advantage for the working class, if attained, lay in the freedom for organization and propaganda which it conferred, not in the provision of an instrument by which the social revolution might be carried out. There was certainly an implied elitism in this attitude; Marx and his associates were convinced that they knew what was good for the workers, and indeed for society as a whole, but the masses were too ignorant, too preoccupied with the daily struggle to earn a living, and too regardless of their own basic interests to remain united and constant over a period of time in the socialist path. Revolution meant that an enlightened and dedicated minority, taking advantage of a favourable conjunction of circumstances and a transient mood of the working masses, would seize power on their behalf and exercise it resolutely without endangering it by submission to the vagaries of democratic elections or of an elected assembly.

But hopes set on a violent dissolution of the social order were disappointed in 1848-9, and the defeat of the Paris Commune in 1871 provided an even greater disappointment. On the other hand, the electoral successes of the German Social Democrats from 1871 onwards showed that the workers would give support at the polls to a party preaching the Marxist social gospel and that universal franchise did render possible a massive parliamentary representation for it. This advance within a constitutional political system raised, however, a problem of a different kind. If political issues were to be decided by counting heads – in so far as they could be so decided under the regime of Bismarck's Germany – how many heads were there to count in the proletariat as distinct from other classes of the population? It was a famous victory if more than a quarter of the voting electors would vote Social Democrat but more than half must give their votes if there were to be a legal democratic majority for a programme of confiscating private property in the means of production. But the increase from more than a quarter to more than a half of the total vote was something the Social Democrats were never able to achieve, and their failure to achieve it was due to fundamental causes; the trouble was that even in a highly industrialized society the proletariat was not a majority of the population. There was a hard core of class-conscious workers with a yearning for socialism and this could not be crushed or suppressed, as was shown by the failure of Bismarck's anti-socialist legislation. But when it came to winning a parliamentary majority, it was found that the class-conscious workers were not by themselves sufficiently numerous and that they could not win over to their side any other substantial section of society for the cause of the abolition of private capital. The Social Democrats obtained an imposing parliamentary representation, but they remained permanently a minority party.

It was one of the theses of Marxism that with the continued development of capitalist industry the proletariat must inevitably become a majority of the population because not only independent artisans but also smaller business men would be driven to the wall by the larger capitalist enterprises and pushed down into the ranks of the wage-earning class. Capital would be concentrated in fewer and fewer hands while the proletariat became more and more numerous. At the same time the proportion of the urban to the rural population would continually increase until the great bulk of the people would be town-dwellers, and in the countryside both peasant proprietors and independently producing tenant farmers would be swept away by large estates using machinery and employing wage labour in agriculture as in industry. Both in town and country, therefore, the rich few would be increasingly differentiated in contrast to the poverty-stricken mass of wage-earners. Nor would the condition of the latter be improved by the increased production of wealth, for the system would never be able to give full and regular employment to all the available workers, and competition for jobs would continually hold down wages close to subsistence level; indeed, conditions for the workers under capitalism would tend to become worse, and not better, as technology advanced and machinery was more and more substituted for manual labour.

This picture of industrial society was one that could carry conviction in the 1840s. The industrial working class was large and becoming larger; it worked long hours for low wages and lived for the most part in appalling slum conditions; it had not yet either trade unions or a parliamentary franchise with which to advance its interests. It was not unreasonable to foresee its future in terms of increasing numbers and aggravated misery. The overwhelming numbers and extreme poverty of the proletariat would give them the advantage whether with or without a parliamentary franchise, for if there were to be free democratic elections the proletariat, as the great majority of the people, would necessarily prevail in them, and if not, its sheer weight of numbers would give it the prospect of ultimate victory over even the most thorough armed repression organized by the ruling capitalist class.

Social evolution in Europe during the later nineteenth century did not, however, follow the course which Marx and Engels anticipated. Society did not become more and more sharply divided between an ever smaller number of the very rich and an ever larger number of the very poor. Great fortunes continued to be made in capitalist enterprise, and wealthy families were not yet curbed by heavy income taxes and death duties, as they were to be in the twentieth century, but the middle classes were not being wiped out, as Marx expected them to be; on the contrary, although old-fashioned craftsmen continued to be swallowed up by the expansion of mechanized industry, all kinds of new small enterprises sprang up for the market created by the new economy, the holding of stocks and shares became increasingly widespread, and the rapidly increasing class of 'white-collar workers' or 'salariat' did not, with rare exceptions, feel any sense of solidarity with the wage-earning proletariat. Even among the manual workers themselves, there was no longer the extreme poverty and destitution which had been characteristic of their condition during the first half of the century, and there was an increasing differentiation of grades, the highest of which reached a level of relative prosperity; a rapidly increasing degree of trade union organization enabled workers to obtain higher wages and better conditions of work while parliamentary franchise made it possible for them to obtain protective legislation and various social services through political action, whether through a party of their own or by making their votes available for bidding by rival parties of the bourgeoisie. All this tended to modify the state of affairs in which workers had nothing to lose but their chains, and to alleviate that mood of desperation on which the preachers of revolution had counted to bring the workers into the streets when the time came. Men whose condition was improving and who could reasonably hope for further improvement in the future without a total change in the order of society were inclined to concern themselves with the pursuit of limited and partial gains and to postpone the effort to attain wider and more fundamental objectives. In the historical era from 1871 to 1914 this was the general tendency of working-class movements in Western Europe.

Marx and Engels adapted their practical political tactics, but not their basic doctrine, to the new trend, with the result that there was an increasing divergence between theory and practice in what came to be known as Marxism. Marx was quick to realize after 1850 that the kind of revolutionary capture of power of which he had dreamed before the events of 1848 was not a practical proposition, and in consequence he dissociated himself more and more from the type of elitist revolutionary plotting which was identified particularly with the name of Blanqui. Since the later Marx so strongly repudiated conspiratorial adventurism, his followers have been at pains to show that he never at any time trod such a path, but the historical record makes it clear that between 1843 and 1850 his outlook was formed by the Jacobin-Babeuvist tradition and that he believed in a revolution which would be carried through by insurgent proletarians, but planned and led by a small secretly organized and self-appointed group. The League of Communists was such a conspiratorial elite, and if we suppose that the events of 1848 had taken a different course, if we imagine that the Prussian monarchy had been not merely intimidated, but overthrown, by the uprising in Berlin, and that in the ensuing confusion the Communists had gained power, if only for a short time, they would have been even fewer in relation to the people of Prussia at that time than were the Bolsheviks in relation to the Russian people in 1917. But in fact, of course, nothing of the kind happened, and Marx moved away from a form of activity which had proved so unrewarding. He came more and more to believe that the aim of practical political action should be the creation of mass organizations of the working class, not of secret societies to plan armed insurrections, but of political parties with the widest possible membership to lead the workers to the polls. Such concentration on peaceful, constitutional action need not in theory be permanent; it was not incompatible with the use of the new type of party organization for a forcible capture of power at some future date. Thus Marx was able in his lifetime to combine a doctrine for which irreconcilable class conflict and violent revolution were fundamental with a tactic which preferred gradualist, non-violent, parliamentary forms of action, and, as we have seen, by 1895, a few years after the death of Marx, Engels was contemplating this situation with the most lively satisfaction. The German Social Democratic Party at its congress held in Erfurt in 1892 had explicitly adopted Marxist theory as the basis of its political programme, but its practice with every year that passed was less concerned with revolution and more with minor gains within the framework of the existing social order.

By the end of the nineteenth century indeed the German Social Democrats, the largest and most highly organized of the working-class parties in Europe, had become a party of non-revolution, yet they were still paying lip-service to the creed of the *Communist Manifesto*. There were some individuals within the party, notably Bernstein, who did not like the discrepancy between theory and practice, and proposed to 'revise' Marxist theory so as to bring it more into line with the assumptions the party was actually making in its practical politics. Bernstein, according to a recent historian of Marxism[1]

... thought Marxism would do better without its Hegelian background; he believed that recent advances in economic theory made it impossible to hold any longer to the labour theory of value; he had doubts about the 'materialist conception of history'; he thought the coming of socialism desirable, but perhaps not inevitable; he could see no evidence of the impoverishment of the working class which Marx had predicted; and he said that bourgeois liberal society had created many things worth preserving.

But the Social Democratic Party would have none of Bernstein's proposed innovations. At their congresses at Hanover in 1899 and at Dresden in 1903 they firmly rejected 'revisionism' and reaffirmed Marxist orthodoxy. Marxism had already become a dogmatic religion in which the claim to be 'scientific' was not deemed to require any adjustment either to a social reality different from that of the 1840s or to the development of the social sciences since that time. There was an adjustment, but it was effected in the field of practice and not of theory, in a manner not unlike that adopted by Christians in adjusting their faith to the world of business competition and political struggle. The revolution which would bring socialism to mankind had become for the leaders of the Social Democrats a far-off divine (or rather materialistically predetermined) event, which was an object of faith, but not of immediate expectation, and their attitude towards it resembled that of the Church of England vicar who, when questioned by a lady of his congregation about the Second Coming of Christ, replied 'It will certainly occur, but not, I trust, in our time.'

If Marxism thus came to stand for non-revolution in the country from which Marx and Engels had themselves come, it was no stronger as a revolutionary force elsewhere in Western Europe. In England it never had

1. John Plamenatz, *German Marxism and Russian Communism*, p. 171.

much influence; the labour movement was slow in detaching itself from left-wing liberalism, and when it did so, it showed a disposition for pragmatic and non-revolutionary politics hardly touched by theoretical speculation. English thinking was predominantly empiricist and allergic to Hegel, therefore also to Marx. In France the revolutionary tradition seemed to have burnt itself out with the Paris Commune of 1871; bitter experience had taught the French proletariat that in a crisis of arms it would find all other classes of society arrayed against it. Marxism was more acceptable in France than in England – though the French had never really taken to Hegel – and the French Socialist Party as constituted after the catastrophe of 1871 was under strong Marxist influence, but this now meant that, as in Germany, it was pursuing the peaceful parliamentary path. The Syndicalists, who formed a large element among the French Socialists, tried to get the best of both worlds; they imagined a general strike which would bring about the collapse of capitalism without either a parliamentary majority or a victory on the barricades, but this general strike soon became as much a vision of the far future as the triumphant *coup de force* for which it was meant to be a substitute. The Anarchists, followers of Proudhon and Bakunin, whose theoretical dissent had given so much trouble to Marx, remained a distinct sect still believing in violence, and reminding the world of their existence by occasional assassinations, but they were not formidable, except in Spain, which was only marginal in the politics of Europe. But there was one country where at the end of the nineteenth century pressures for revolution were not subsiding, but growing; where Hegel had been received with great honour and Marx had followed, and where an important political group was going back beyond Social Democracy to the Marxism of the *Communist Manifesto*. That country was Russia and it was there that a revolution, such as Marx had envisaged in 1848, was actually to take place.

3. Marxism and the Russian Narodniks

In Western Europe Marxism was only one among several varieties of socialist political thought, but none of the other varieties was able to oppose it with a doctrine of comparable intellectual appeal. In Russia, however, it encountered a rival form of socialist faith, which not only proved a most formidable competitor, but had in the long run a profound influence on the development of Marxism itself, so that the 'Leninist' variant of Marxism, which after the Russian Revolution of 1917 became the official ideology of the new Soviet regime, showed characteristics which could only be traced to non-Marxist origins.

This rival doctrine was that of the Narodniks or Populists, and its main distinguishing feature lay in its 'peasant orientation'. The *narod* or 'people', to whose cause they dedicated themselves, meant primarily the peasantry, and this corresponded to the fact that in nineteenth-century Russia the peasants were the great majority of the population. Compared with most of Western Europe, Russia had remained essentially an agrarian country, and this was synonymous with its general economic backwardness. At the beginning of the nineteenth century less than five per cent of the population of Russia lived in towns, and at the end of the century not more than twenty per cent. The vast continental land mass of Russia which rendered it so difficult for a foreign conqueror to subdue it – as Charles XII and Napoleon had found to their cost – also created economic conditions which, before the development of railway transport, were adverse to commerce and industry, and even the river system of the Russian empire was for the most part inconvenient for foreign trade, for the largest river of European Russia flowed to the landlocked Caspian, while the great rivers of Siberia led only to the Arctic Ocean. With its immense territory and numerous population, providing a formidable military manpower in so far as it could be trained, mobilized and supplied in time of war, Russia became one of the Great Powers of Europe, but with weaker economic foundations and a more archaic social structure than the Western members of that select group. Nor were the economic and social peculiarities of Russia merely a matter of the survival of institutions which had been superseded in the West; in the sixteenth and seventeenth centuries, when the medieval institutions of feudal military tenure and peasant serfdom were declining in the West, they were being re-created in the special conditions of the environment of Russia. Western Europe had by 1500 a wholly settled population; it had frontiers between states but no 'Frontier' in the later American sense of vast almost uninhabited hinterlands whither people could migrate and settle virtually beyond the jurisdiction of the established government. Russia, on the other hand, had such unoccupied lands along its borders both to the east in Siberia and to the south towards the Black Sea, the Caucasus and the Caspian. In these circumstances Russia had to cope with the peculiar problem of peasant 'flight'. To maintain its armies and its revenues and to carry on the administration of its enormous territory the Russian state relied on a class of nobles who held land on condition of state service, military or civil, and these landed estates had to be cultivated if they were to support their holders. But if the peasants were pressed too hard for rents and taxes they might emigrate to the empty lands of the frontier zones and become 'free settlers' or join the semi-independent communities of Cossacks who lived a life which combined hunting, stock-raising and banditry. A landlord might thus suddenly find his estate untenanted, and it was for this reason that it became customary for Russian nobles to reckon their wealth, not in the number of their acres, but in the number of their 'souls', and the state did its best to ensure them a sufficient number of 'souls' by binding them legally to the estates of the 'serving' nobility. The system of serfdom, as it existed in Russia in the eighteenth century, was not of medieval origin, but a creation of the previous two hundred years. In the same way, the Russian village community known as the *mir*, which was responsible for taxes and allocated land among peasant families, was not an institution surviving from ancient times, but a device of state policy closely connected with the institution of serfdom itself and designed to bind the peasantry even more closely to the performance of their obligations.

Peter the Great in his reconstruction of the Russian state did not move towards the mitigation of the system of serfdom, but on the contrary intensified it, for in his task of building up Russian power he was in desperate need of both money and soldiers, and ever more onerous burdens were laid on the peasant masses. But the nobility also, despite the great rewards which they might gain in the service of the state, were not let off lightly by Peter; their service was for life and the obligation was rigorously enforced. It was not until 1762 that Peter III released the nobility from compulsory state service; after that date they continued to seek careers in the army or the state administration if they so desired, but they could, if they wished, live in idleness on their incomes as landlords, or rather owners of serfs. Serfdom continued in Russia for almost a hundred years after the release of the nobility from their obligations of state service, and this fact had an effect on political thinking in Russia which has seldom been adequately appreciated. In Western Europe the concept of feudal landholding as a conditional tenure had gradually passed out of social consciousness and been absorbed by the idea of absolute private property in land, but in Russia, just because the principle of obligations inseparable from landholding had prevailed so much later in time, the abrupt conversion of service tenures into unconditional private owner-ship was more sharply challenged. The rumour spread among the peasants that Peter III had decreed the eman-cipation of the serfs as well as the release of the nobles from compulsory service, but that the nobles had sup-pressed the document and deposed the Tsar in order to keep possessions to which they were not entitled; this was an idea which contributed largely to the great peasant insurrection led by Pugachev in 1773. Even after the suppression of this uprising the peasant serfs continued to question the right of the nobles to the ownership of the land, and their attitude was expressed in the curious saying 'We are yours, but the land is ours'. Nor was it only the peasants who were influenced by the idea that the rights of the nobility were illegitimate after the abolition of the duties on which they had previously been conditional; doubts haunted many of the land-owners themselves, and it was this state of affairs which produced the remarkable number of 'conscience-stricken' individuals in the Russian nobility of the nineteenth century. This was not because members of the Russian upper classes were so much more liable to qualms of social conscience than their counterparts in Western Europe, but because their assurance of the validity of their property rights was so much less, in view of the recent date of their establishment as a landowning class in the full sense of the word. They might soon have rid themselves of any feelings of embarrassment about the justice of the legislation of 1762, but within a generation they were, as a 'westernized' aristocracy who spoke and read French in preference to their own language, being exposed to the currents of liberal and radical thought emanating from Western Europe. It is this situation which explains the extraordinary prominence of indi-viduals of aristocratic origin in the revolutionary move-ment in nineteenth-century Russia. First the leaders of the Decembrists and later Herzen, Ogarev, Bakunin, Tkachev and Kropotkin all came from the ranks of the nobility – a feature without parallel in Western Europe, where the pioneers of political radicalism were nearly all of urban middle-class origin. In Russia also in the later years of the nineteenth century there emerged revolutionary leaders who were not of noble birth – Chernyshevsky, Nechaiev and those who were later to form the Russian Social Democratic Party – but in the perspective of the nineteenth century as a whole, and particularly in the ideological formation of Russian Populism, the aristocratic element is of outstanding importance and it contributed to the Russian revolutionary tradition certain characteristics which, in a roundabout way, were to be transmitted to the party destined to conquer power in Russia in 1917.

Social radicalism in Russia around the middle of the nineteenth century was bound to concern itself primarily with the agrarian problem in view of the great numerical preponderance of the peasantry over all other classes of the population and the persistence of serfdom as an institution until 1861. But the tendency to preoccupation with the peasantry was greatly strengthened by the influence of the 'conscience-stricken' nobles for whom the question of the ownership of serfs and of income from peasant labour was necessarily in the forefront of all social problems. In 1861 serfdom was abolished by the 'Tsar Liberator' Alexander II, but the social tensions in the countryside remained, and were in some ways even aggravated, for the nobility retained much of the land as private estates and the land which was allotted to the peasants was burdened with redemption payments which were to be extended over a long period of time. Thus it was in the 1860s and 1870s, when serfdom was already a thing of the past, that the agitation for a radical transformation of Russian rural society reached its climax. It came to be combined with a socialist ideal, partly because of the vogue of socialist thinking among Russian intellectuals at the time, but mainly because of a historical misinterpretation of the institution of the village *mir* mentioned above. The *mir* was supposed to be a survival of a primitive communism among the Russian peasantry and as such it was regarded as a foundation on which a collectivist economic order could be built in the countryside. The cravings of the Russian peasant to own land as his private property and sell its produce as he pleased were ignored or minimized, and it was held that because of the *mir* he was naturally a socialist, having retained the pristine virtues of collective living which in the West had long since been obliterated by the inroads of economic individualism. The economic backwardness of Russia was thus no handicap, but a positive advantage for the attainment of socialism, since Russian society, having been less deeply corrupted by capitalism, could be more rapidly regenerated than that of the West. Indeed Russia could arrive before the West in the Socialist Utopia and thus become the teacher and model for the West instead of the pupil and imitator which she had been since Peter the Great had forcibly dragged her from her old Muscovite-Byzantine cultural seclusion and made her a part of Europe. There were overtones of Russian nationalism in this way of thinking and some kinship with the Slavophiles, who denounced the cultural influence of the West and claimed that Russia had a unique civilization of her own which had been outraged and deformed by the reforms of Peter. The Slavophiles like the Narodniks idealized the Russian peasantry, but whereas the former saw it as the preserver of the traditional values of Orthodox Christianity, repudiated since the time of Peter by a secularist and sceptical upper class, the Narodniks saw it as the class which could and would create an entirely new society. The Slavophile romantics looked back to a golden age of the past, whereas the Narodniks looked forward to a glorious future which they felt to be near at hand.

This new society was to be brought to birth by violent revolution; under the autocracy of the Tsar, with its army and police to maintain the established order, there did not appear to be any other way of effecting radical social change. But about the form of this revolution and the methods by which it was to be promoted there was plenty of controversy. Russia had a tradition of *jacquerie*; there had been many local peasant revolts and three large-scale ones since 1600 – those led by Bolotnikov and Stenka Razin in the seventeenth century and that of Pugachev in the eighteenth. All three had been suppressed after temporary success; all had been marked by extreme destructiveness and by wholesale massacres of the landed gentry. Their great weakness had been in their lack of clearly formulated aims or of any leadership other than that of individual adventurers who were little more than brigands. The Narodniks believed that the explosive force that was still latent in the oppressed peasantry could be harnessed and guided by the socialist intelligentsia so that in another great insurrection it would not dissipate itself in blind excesses but would accomplish a complete transformation of society. There were, however, differences of opinion about the parts to be played in the revolution by the peasant insurrection and the educated guidance. The more optimistic of the Narodniks saw the peasant masses as ripe for revolution and capable of creating the new society by themselves, the function of the revolutionary intellectuals being merely to provide an initial impulse. The less optimistic, on the other hand, had serious doubts about the capacity of the peasants to carry through a social revolution on their own account; their poverty, ignorance and inertia disqualified them for co-ordinated and sustained action, so that they would need to be directed by a small conspiratorially organized group of ideologically enlightened and fully dedicated revolutionaries until the new order of things was finally established.

This latter trend in the Narodnik movement, with the elitism it implied, had certain affinities with the revolutionary tradition represented in Western Europe by Babeuf, Buonarroti and Blanqui. Secret organization was always unavoidable under conditions in which the open political activity of radical sects was suppressed by the power of the state, and in Russia there was no liberty for such agitation before 1905. But elitism was carried further in Russia than in Western Europe and it was no accident that its two most notable exponents, Ogarev and Tkachev – both of whom had a profound influence on Lenin[1] – came from the nobility. It was easier for political thinkers of this social origin to renounce their claims to unearned income than to get rid of the idea that they were the natural leaders of the uneducated and mainly illiterate masses who could accomplish nothing without them. From this milieu also came a strong belief in the efficacy of conspiratorial methods arising out of relatively recent historical experience. During the eighteenth century Russia had witnessed an extraordinary series of 'palace revolutions' to which the annals of monarchy in contemporary Western Europe afforded no parallel. In the words of a historian of Russia:[2]

> With Peter the Great's aristocracy at their head and the army behind them, the regiments of the Guards made or unmade the emperors or empresses of Russia from Catherine I to Alexander I. It was they who inaugurated the era of palace revolutions. Throughout the melodramatic changes and chances of court intrigue in the Russia of Peter's successors the threads of conspiracy around the throne always led back to the Guards' barracks in St Petersburg.

In the eighteenth century there had been no purpose in these *coups d'état* beyond the ascendancy of this or that faction of the nobility, but in the unsuccessful Decembrist rising of 1825 there had been a programme of social change, including liberation of the serfs, and it was proposed to set up a dictatorship to carry it out. By the middle of the nineteenth century it was no longer possible

1. See S. V. Utechin, *Russian Political Thought*, pp. 124–7 and 217.
2. Richard Charques, *A History of Russia*, p. 99.

to hope that senior officers of the regular army could be involved in plans for a social revolution, but it was still hoped that a secretly organized conspiratorial group would be able to promote not only a widespread peasant insurrection, but also mutinies among the troops who would be sent to suppress it. Ogarev held that the revolutionaries should concentrate their energies on propaganda at the rural fairs, where peasants gathered together on certain occasions from wide regions, and in garrison towns where they could make converts among soldiers. Tkachev formulated even more precisely the function of the revolutionary elite:

The revolutionary minority, having freed the people from the yoke of fear of the powers that be, opens up for it an opportunity for it to reveal its destructive revolutionary force, and leaning upon this force, skilfully directing it towards annihilation of the immediate enemies of the revolution, the minority destroys the latter's protective fortress and deprives them of all means of resistance and counteraction. Then, making use of its strength and authority, it introduces new, progressively communist elements into the conditions of the people's life.

Both the less and the more elitist sections of the Narodnik movement tried out their preferred methods in practice in the 1870s. Those who believed that the peasant masses needed only a little preaching to stimulate them to make a revolution of overwhelming force sought to provide the impulse by 'going to the people'; hundreds of young men and women, mostly from wealthy families, but dedicated to lives of voluntary poverty, went into the villages to spread the new gospel of social revolution. But in spite of the widespread discontent in the countryside they achieved very little; the peasants were generally distrustful and hostile towards these strange missionaries from another class and frequently betrayed them to the police. After the failure of this enterprise it was the turn of the believers in direct action to show what they could do. They mounted a campaign of terrorist acts against officials of the Tsarist government and for a time achieved a considerable success in intimidating and demoralizing the guardians of the established order; nobody seemed to be safe from the bombs and pistols of the 'nihilists', as they came to be called. The campaign culminated in the assassination of the Tsar Alexander II in 1881, but this success was the beginning of the end for those who promoted it; there was a widespread revulsion of feeling against the terrorists, and the government launched a well organized counter-offensive, using *agents provocateurs* to penetrate the ranks of the revolutionaries. Their losses were so heavy that the idea of individual assassinations as a means for the overthrow of the established order was discredited and many of the Narodniks gave way to despair. Their disappointment was aggravated by historical researches which proved that the *mir* was no survival of an ancient collectivism in Russian rural society, but a device of the Tsarist state for more effectively controlling the peasantry; it had been retained after the abolition of serfdom in 1861 as the best instrument for collecting the annuities owed by the peasants for the land which had been transferred to them.

Into the intellectual vacuum created by the collapse of Populism Marxism made its way with increasing success in the closing years of the nineteenth century. It preached the doctrine that revolutionary salvation was to be found not in the peasantry but in the industrial proletariat, which was now for the first time, from about 1890 onwards, becoming a really considerable factor in Russian society; modern large-scale industry arrived late in Russia, but when it did, it developed rapidly with corresponding increases in the numbers of urban wage-workers. It was under the banner of Marxism, and not that of Populism, that the socialist revolution was destined to triumph in Russia in 1917. Yet there remained a twofold legacy of Populism which is of crucial importance for the understanding of the theory and practice of Communism in the modern world. The Narodnik orientation on the peasantry as the main revolutionary class was repudiated by the Marxists, yet the strategy of worker – peasant alliance as worked out by Lenin was something of which Marx himself would not have dreamed, and the agrarian guerrilla revolution of China led by Mao Tse-tung came even nearer to the Narodnik hope. Even more fully did the elitism so prevalent among the Narodniks influence the development of Marxism in Russia, so that Communism as a creed after 1917 sought to promote a political system of which the central feature was the dictatorial rule of a single tightly organized and disciplined party.

4. Lenin

The writings of Marx were known in Russia by legal publication from the year 1872, when the first volume of *Das Kapital* appeared in a Russian translation. It got past the Russian censorship because it was classified as a treatise on economics and could not therefore be politically dangerous as were the works of John Stuart Mill and other exponents of democratic thought.

Even before 1872 Russian revolutionary theorists had been acquainted with Marxism and had been influenced by it, but it appeared to be inapplicable in so essentially an agrarian country as Russia was until after 1880. The Populists were, as we have seen, the main element in the Russian revolutionary movement between 1872 and 1881, but they lost ground rapidly after the assassination of the Tsar Alexander II in the latter year, and by the year 1887, when Vladimir Ulyanov, later to be known as Lenin, became a student in the University of Kazan, Marxism had already begun to sway the minds of the *avant-garde* of the Russian intelligentsia.

Lenin was born at Simbirsk on the Volga in eastern Russia of a curiously mixed ancestry. His paternal grandfather was a Russian tailor in Astrakhan who married a Kalmuk woman – whence came probably his markedly 'mongoloid' features; his maternal grandmother was German and his maternal grandfather, who bore the name of Blank, was according to one version a converted Jew from Odessa – though this has been strongly denied. It seems to have been Blank at any rate who established the fortune of the Ulyanov family, for, having made money through the practice of medicine, he purchased a country estate at Kokushkino, and this later passed to his son-in-law Ilya Ulyanov, who in 1863 married his daughter, Maria Alexandrovna, the mother of Lenin. Even before making his financially advantageous marriage Ilya had come up in the world; having acquired a university education, he became a teacher of science and mathematics, and in 1869 he received an official appointment as Inspector of Schools for the province of Simbirsk. Lenin spent the early years of his life at Simbirsk in the circumstances of a well-to-do Russian home with occasional excursions to the estate at Kokushkino, where his grandfather had once owned the peasants as serfs.

Before his death in 1886 Ilya had been so successful in his official career that he received an appointment as State Councillor, which conferred on him a rank of nobility. As far as is known, he never had the idea of demolishing the social and political system under which he had prospered so well. But his son Alexander, by four years the elder brother of the future Lenin, was drawn into the revolutionary movement as a student in the University of St Petersburg and took part in a plot to assassinate the Tsar Alexander III in 1887. The plot was discovered and Alexander Ulyanov and his fellow-conspirators were arrested; he was sentenced to death and hanged at the age of twenty-one.

Alexander was still a Narodnik, but had already before his death been attracted towards Marxism. There is no evidence that Vladimir had yet any definite political views at the time of his brother's execution. But that event made him emotionally a revolutionary even though without any clear doctrinal commitment. Within a year of Alexander's death he was involved in a student demonstration in Kazan which caused him to be both arrested by the police and expelled from the University. He was soon released from prison, but condemned to a period of enforced residence on the family estate at Kokushkino. Later the family moved to Samara, where for four years Vladimir privately studied law and then applied for official permission to take law examinations without being a member of a university. The concession was granted to 'Nobleman Vladimir Ulyanov' and he qualified professionally as a lawyer. In 1893 he went to live in St Petersburg.

He had already begun to study Marxist literature in Samara, and in St Petersburg he at once joined a circle of enthusiastic adherents of the new doctrine. In this circle he soon made an impression by his combination of great theoretical erudition with skill and vigour in debate. According to a memoir by someone who knew him at that time[1] he was noted for 'his undeviating and uncompromising attitude towards principles amounting to, as we soon began to say, "stone-hardness"', but also 'relatively very flexible on questions of day-to-day tactics'.

In 1893 there was not yet any regularly organized Social Democratic Party in Russia, but there were a number of more or less secret study circles inside the country which maintained tenuous communications with a group of Russian exiles in France and Switzerland headed by the Marxist writer Plekhanov. The exiles were of course free to express and discuss their political ideas in a way whch was impossible inside Russia, but they could only exert influence in Russia to the extent that they were able to smuggle their writings across the Russian frontier. The practical problem that confronted the Marxists under conditions of Russian censorship and police repression was that of creating an organization which would both co-ordinate the various centres inside Russia and facilitate the introduction of propaganda literature from abroad. The first effort was made from within Russia and took the form of a congress held secretly in Minsk in 1898 to found an 'All-Russian Social Democratic Labour Party'. Most of the delegates were, however, arrested by the police soon afterwards, and no effective organization was set up. This situation left the

1. Vasili Starkov, memoir printed in *Krasnaya Nov*, November 1925, and quoted by Louis Fischer, *The Life of Lenin*, p. 20.

way open for the exiles to try their hand at organizing the movement, and this was undertaken in 1900, when a newspaper called *Iskra* ('The Spark') was started in Munich; it was intended both to provide ideological direction and to give organizational unity to the groups inside Russia, for the agents who would distribute the paper inside Russia would form an underground network through which a central control could be exercised over all true believers.

This idea was specially Lenin's, though at first he was only one of six persons who formed the editorial board of *Iskra*. He had only recently arrived in Western Europe after a period of imprisonment and exile in Siberia. He had been arrested for illegal political activities in December 1895. In prison he wrote part of a book on the development of capitalism in Russia; in Siberia, where he lived in a village within sight of the Sayan mountains on what was then the frontier of the Chinese empire, he lived comfortably, married Nadezhda Krupskaya, a schoolteacher who had also been exiled to Siberia for subversive activities, and carried on a correspondence with Marxist leaders both in Russia and in Europe. After Lenin had himself become the ruler of Russia, political prisoners were not to have such an easy time of it, but at the end of the nineteenth century, although the Russian government was still an unqualified autocracy, the rigour of state repression of dissent had been considerably softened, at least for persons of high education and social rank.

Lenin left Russia after his term of banishment to Sibera had expired and now devoted himself to a campaign against a trend which he regarded as most dangerous for the Social Democratic movement in Russia. This was the heresy of 'economism', the idea that Marxists should encourage the industrial workers to concentrate their energies on immediate economic goals – higher wages and better conditions of work – leaving political aims to be pursued as a consequence of this activity. For

Lenin this meant in effect an abandonment of the objective of socialism in favour of piecemeal improvements which would never alter the fundamental character of the economic system. In his attack on 'economism' Lenin expressed his disbelief in the capacity of the proletariat to originate a genuinely revolutionary action by itself alone. 'The history of all countries', he declared, 'bears witness that the working class by virtue of its own powers alone is capable solely of developing a trade union consciousness, that is the conviction of the necessity of uniting in trade unions, carrying on a struggle against employers, or putting pressure on the government to pass this or that law to the advantage of the workers.' But the political class consciousness which would drive on the workers to make a real social revolution could only be brought to them from outside, that is to say, from an elite of ideologically qualified revolutionaries. In this attitude the Marxist conception of the destiny of the proletariat as the revolutionary class is combined wth the elitism of the Narodniks; the industrial workers may be more promising material than the peasants for the construction of a socialist order, but they also need to be guided and directed; if left to themselves and leaders whom they may freely choose, they will get nowhere.

This elitism, this paternal and authoritarian attitude towards the class in the name of which the social revolution was to be made, affected Lenin's conception of the Social Democratic Party itself as the instrument of political action. If it were to enlarge its membership without exacting disciplined political work from its members, if it were to become a large body of men bound together only by a nominal adherence to certain abstract principles, the genuine dedicated revolutionaries in the Party would be swamped by a mass of lukewarm followers drifting towards 'economism' and compromise with the existing social order. Lenin expressed his view of what the Party ought to be like in his book entitled *What Is To Be Done?*, published in Geneva in 1902. In this he argued[2] that 'no revolutionary movement can be durable without a stable organization of leaders which preserves continuity'; that 'the broader the mass which is spontaneously drawn into the struggle ... the more urgent is the necessity for such an organization'; and that 'such an organization must consist mainly of people who are professionally engaged in revolutionary activities'.

The 'professional revolutionaries' of whom Lenin wrote were no mere products of his imagination; they already existed as a type in Russia. They did not earn a living apart from their political activities, partly because they gave their whole time to the cause, and partly also because they were usually on the move from place to place in order to escape from the attentions of the police. For their livelihood a few of them depended on their own property or allowances from their families – Lenin himself received money from his mother – but more often they relied on Party funds raised by a variety of means, which might even include armed robberies. Cut off from all normal social life, living always in danger of arrest and pursued even abroad by police spies, and associating mainly with his own kind, the dedicated professional revolutionary became a distinct type of human being, austere and resolute, but secretive, suspicious and skilled in every sort of deceit and dissimulation, convinced that nothing in human life mattered compared with politics and that men must be saved or damned according to the exact definition of their political beliefs. This type had already emerged among the Narodniks; it now came to the fore in the Russian section of a movement which in Western Europe was moving further and further away from conspiratorial techniques towards mass party activity under conditions of political democracy. It could, of course, be claimed that the special situation in Russia, by 1902 the only European country except Turkey to be without any form of national parlia-

2. V. I. Lenin, *What is to be done?* Translated by S. V. and Patricia Utechin, Oxford, 1963, p. 144.

mentary representation, required for the time being a type of party organization such as Lenin postulated. But, although Lenin advocated the overthrow of the autocracy and the attainment of political liberty as an immediate political goal, it is clear from the pages of *What Is To Be Done?* that he did not regard his organizational model as something that would be rendered superfluous by the advent of political democracy. On the contrary he considered it would be even more necessary in a period when everyone would have a vote and be free to use it. If a majority of the industrial proletariat was liable to be led astray by 'economism', with the proletariat itself only a small minority of the total population, the only prospect for socialism lay in a party of rigorously selected and highly disciplined membership which would know how to act in a crisis without regard to majorities either in the country at large or even in the ranks of the working class. If Russia had to wait until the proletariat was a majority of the population and had itself freely decided to give priority to the task of socialist transformation, Lenin did not see how socialism could come in his lifetime. But by temperament he was not inclined to work merely for a 'far-off divine event'; he wanted socialist revolution and he wanted it soon. In his impatience he was out of line with most of the other leaders of the Russian Social Democrats at that time. As Leonard Schapiro puts it: [3]

Whether they realized it or not, Plekhanov, Potresov and Akselrod were still thinking of a revolution in two stages – the bourgeois and socialist stages. Lenin was, though perhaps not consciously, looking towards an immediate socialist revolution.

At the Second Congress of the Russian Social Democratic Party, which was convened in Brussels in July 1903, Lenin tried to get the constitution of the Party framed in accordance with a draft which he had prepared, but he ran into serious opposition, and on an

3. L. Schapiro, *The Communist Party of the Soviet Union*, p. 46.

issue he regarded as crucial he was defeated by twenty-eight votes to twenty-three. But the opposing majority included the five delegates of the Jewish Socialist Party, known as the Bund, which claimed autonomy within the Russian Party, and two representatives of the 'economists'. When a majority vote denied the Bund the autonomy it sought, all seven delegates withdrew from the Congress, and Lenin was left with a majority of the votes that remained. In this way his faction came to be known as 'the majority' or Bolsheviks, while his opponents were styled 'the minority' or Mensheviks. The classification was by no means conclusive, for it is very doubtful whether Lenin could at any time between 1903 and 1917 have confirmed his claim to leadership by a counting of heads of Party members. The Mensheviks retained a strong following and were able to prevent Lenin from getting his own way altogether in the Party. But to get his own way was always what Lenin was determined to do, and if he could not convert the Mensheviks to his own way of thinking, he was prepared to split the Party so as to have an organization composed entirely of his own followers. The split did not come immediately; the two factions continued nominally to coexist for nine years as groups within a single party, and various attempts were made to reconcile them, but in 1912 the breach became final, and Bolsheviks and Mensheviks became to all intents and purposes separate parties. Both, however, continued to claim the title of Social Democrat until in 1919, after the capture of political power in Russia, the Bolsheviks renamed themselves the Communist Party; this was more than a mere matter of words, for by the change of title the Bolsheviks repudiated all connexion with the contemporary Social Democratic parties of Central Europe and proclaimed their historical continuity with the original League of Communists which had produced the *Communist Manifesto* in 1848.

In 1903, however, there were not yet any Communists; there were only quarrelling factions of Social Democrats.

The quarrel did not then appear to be very relevant for practical politics, for there was nothing to suggest that a collapse of the Tsardom was imminent. But in 1904 Russia was at war with Japan and a succession of naval and military defeats deeply discredited the Tsarist government, resulting in a general demand for a parliamentary constitution in which bourgeois liberals, Narodniks (now reorganized to form the Social Revolutionary Party) and Social Democrats could join forces for the time being. The slaughter in St Petersburg on 'Bloody Sunday' in January 1905, when troops opened fire on a workers' demonstration, was followed by a revolutionary upheaval which shook the regime to its foundations. Everywhere in Russia there were strikes, demonstrations, riots and assassinations of officials; in the countryside there were peasant risings with pillage and burning of mansions of the nobility. On 13 September a council (soviet) of workers' delegates was set up in St Petersburg, and similar councils came into being in a number of other Russian cities. The first chairman of the St Petersburg Soviet was arrested in November and was succeeded by a fiery revolutionary orator who went under the pseudonym of Trotsky. Almost simultaneously Lenin returned to Russia and assumed the leadership of the Bolsheviks in the capital.

Trotsky was an admirer of Lenin, but not a follower; a man of highly original views and independent mind, he did not at this time consider himself either a Bolshevik or a Menshevik. Lenin's biographer Louis Fischer thus describes the contrast between the two men in 1905:[4]

Trotsky at this period was primarily a mass-appeal man, Lenin an organization man. Trotsky needed a stage, Lenin an office.... Party ties meant little to Trotsky; he preferred the role of lone wolf outside the pack ... Lenin on the other hand competed feverishly for his party's supremacy over other socialist parties. In fact, however, the Bolsheviks were very

4. L. Fischer, op. cit., p. 51.

weak.... Lenin's role in Russia in 1905 was therefore not primary. His time had not come.

In terms of revolutionary action Lenin did very little in 1905. The armed rising in Moscow which marked the climax of the revolutionary movement was led by Social Revolutionaries, not by Bolsheviks. Lenin's efforts were devoted to building up his own underground organization with a view to the future. Meanwhile the tide turned; by granting a constitution the Tsar appeased and detached the moderates in the revolutionary camp while the end of the war with Japan made available large military forces for repression of the extremists who wanted more than a Duma. As order was restored and police activity against subversion was intensified Lenin came to be increasingly in danger of arrest, and in November 1907 he again left Russia for Western Europe, not to return until after the fall of the Tsardom in 1917. He was not a coward, but he considered that he could lead his party more effectively from Paris or Geneva than from the inside of a Russian prison or a village in Siberia.

The Russia that confronted Lenin after 1905 was no longer the Russia of the beginning of the century; it now possessed a national parliament, even though executive authority remained in the hands of the Tsar and his Ministers, who were not responsible to the Duma. The censorship was relaxed and political parties now competed in the open for public support. Any further progress towards full political democracy could only accentuate the trend towards a state of affairs in which small conspiratorial groups would be replaced by mass parties seeking national electoral majorities. But in such a society what would be the prospects for socialism? The ever more numerous and wealthy middle classes would strive for the further development of capitalism; the peasants, still more than four fifths of the total population, would demand agrarian reform but in order to own the land they tilled as their private property. Even among the industrial workers there was likely to be more effort for higher wages and social services than for state owner-ship of the means of production. In the end no doubt the growth of industry and the proletarianization of the masses would bring about a socialist revolution – no Marxist could but believe that – but the day would be far off, further off than in Western Europe, since capital-ism in Russia was still so much less advanced.

There was only one hope for a revolution of the kind willed by Lenin, and that was a breakdown of the exist-ing regime in Russia which would produce not a free democracy, but political chaos. The upheaval of 1905 had provided glimpses of what was possible, particularly in the violent disorder of the peasant revolts. If the remaining power of the Tsardom with its army and police could be eliminated without a parliamentary democratic regime being able to consolidate its authority, then in that vacuum of government a small group of disciplined and determined men who knew what they wanted would have their hour of opportunity. Lenin did not candidly declare a desire for chaos, for that would be tactically inexpedient, but it was implicit in the formula he coined in 1905 to define his objective: 'a revolutionary-democratic dictatorship of the proletariat and the peasantry'. Such a phrase went far beyond any-thing Marxists had hitherto contemplated in the way of a political alliance with peasants; indeed it savoured of heresy. But Lenin was not forsaking Marxism; he did not really mean that the urban workers should share power with the peasantry, much less give them the deci-sive voice to which their superior numbers would entitle them. The role of the peasantry in Lenin's calculation, as he was to show in 1917, was to be a negative and destructive one; they were to wreck the old social and political order and make such a confusion in Russia that no liberal democratic republic could be set up. Lenin realized from his own observation of what happened in 1905 that the peasants were a force not to be ignored and that they were capable of furious violence; it would not be difficult, given a sufficient weakening of the state authority, to raise the ghosts of Stenka Razin and Pugachev for a new *jacquerie*. But Lenin also saw that the peasants were too dispersed, unorganized, and incoherent to be able to create a new national authority in a period of political disintegration. The 'democratic dictatorship of the workers and peasants' would in practice be one of the workers only, and it would, of course, be exercised by the workers' party, the Bolshevik Social Democrats obedient to the will of Lenin himself.

5. The Capture of Power in Russia

At the beginning of the year 1914 there was no good reason to expect a new revolutionary upheaval in Russia in the near future. The authority of the Tsarist state had been restored after the disturbances of 1905–6 and middle-class discontent had been largely appeased by the grant of a parliamentary constitution which provided a safety-valve for the new political pressures without depriving the Tsar and his Ministers of the ultimate executive power. Moreover, a change of the original electoral law in 1907 had weighted the franchise strongly in favour of the propertied classes and rendered the parliament, known as the Duma, less dangerous to the established order. Among the masses of peasants and workers widespread discontent remained, but it was reduced both by the continued expansion of industry which provided employment for numbers of landless peasants moving from the countryside to the towns and by the agrarian policy initiated by the Prime Minister Stolypin which encouraged the rise of a new class of relatively well-to-do peasant proprietors between the old landowning gentry and the still poverty-stricken peasantry emancipated from serfdom half a century before. Russia was still economically backward compared with Western Europe, but appeared to be moving fairly rapidly away from the old serf-and-landlord pattern of society towards a Western norm. This trend was, as in Western Europe, unfavourable to the advocacy of violent revolutionary methods for the solution of social problems, since it gave increasing numbers of people a stake in social stability and promised redress of grievances by legal means. The new spirit of the times was reflected in a distinct turn of Russian socialist opinion against Lenin manifest at a conference held in Brussels on 16 and 17 July 1914, just a few days before the Austrian ultimatum to Serbia precipitated the international crisis which led to the First World War. The conference had been called by the Bureau of the Socialist International in the hope of reconciling the Bolsheviks, Mensheviks and separate organizations of Russian Polish and Russian Jewish Socialists in order to reunite the Russian Social Democratic Party. The break-up of the Russian Party had become a scandal in the international Socialist movement, and the Bureau of the Socialist International had offered its services as a mediator. The Bolsheviks under Lenin's direction – though he did not himself attend the conference – maintained a completely intransigent attitude, but they were isolated, and it was clear that the sympathies of the Western European Socialists were ranged on the other side. Lenin's influence had indeed begun to decline and with a few more years of international peace would probably have diminished further. But within three weeks of the Brussels conference Europe was at war, and the politics of Social Democrats everywhere were suddenly distracted by the need to take decisions in each country on the question whether or not to support the national effort to win the war. In Marxist theory the working classes of different countries had no conflicting interests which could cause them to go to war; armed struggles between states only arose because of the urges of capitalists in each country to destroy foreign trade rivals, acquire colonies or enlarge protected markets. War was regarded as essentially economic in its motivation, a form of bourgeois competition which went beyond the ordinary non-violent procedures of capitalist exploitation. It followed that Socialists ought not to promote or support it in any way and that they should do all they could in time of peace to prevent it from happening. But if nevertheless war were to break out, what were they to do? Theoretically, if working-class conscripts refused to fight, and if workers in arms factories refused to produce arms, governments could not carry on a war. But what if the workers in country A refused to fight or to work for the war effort while those in country B failed to offer similar opposition to their own government? The result would be not to stop war but merely to make sure that state B would be victorious. The Social Democrats before 1914 never really faced the dilemma involved in the theory of proletarian opposition to war, and when the test came in 1914 the two most important parties of the International, the French and the German, became 'social patriots', that is to say, they put their respective national causes before international proletarian solidarity and supported their own capitalist governments in the waging of the war. In France they saw German troops sweeping across the frontier towards Lille and Paris; in Germany they shuddered at news of Russian Cossacks riding into East Prussia. In Russia, as in France and Germany, there was a surge of patriotic emotion which for the time being rallied the masses round the government, but there was no formal support for the Russian government by the Russian Social Democrats. Their deputies in the Duma, both Bolsheviks and Mensheviks, refused to vote for war credits, and adopted a resolution calling on the international proletariat to terminate the war as soon as possible. In this resolution there was indeed no suggestion of a preference for the defeat of Russia and still less of any action to bring it about. But it was just in this direction that Lenin's fanatical hatred of the Tsardom soon led him. From his exile in Switzerland – whither he had moved from Austria after the outbreak of the war – he proclaimed that Russia's defeat was desirable since it would hasten the collapse of the Tsarist regime. He might equally from Marxist principles have found it desirable that Germany should be defeated, since that would be likely to result in the fall of the Hohenzollerns, but he regarded the Russian autocracy as the worst government in Europe and its elimination was therefore specially to be desired; it would also mean that Russia rather than Germany would lead the way in European revolution, but Lenin, whatever he may have hoped, did not base his thesis on this argument. In any case it had no immediate practical effect except that the Russian police used it as a pretext for arresting the five Bolshevik deputies in the Duma as traitors.

All the European governments that went to war in 1914 expected the struggle to be short and sharp, resulting in a decisive victory for one side or the other. What nobody imagined was a war lasting for more than four years. Initially it was fought with the peace-time regular armies enlarged by calling in reservists and with stocks of arms already built up. But as it was prolonged month after month and year after year, problems of an internal economic and political order became no less crucial for the warring governments than those of strategy and diplomacy. It was necessary to keep up the morale of armies into which new recruits were continually being poured to fill the gaps due to enormous casualties, to maintain supplies of food and essential commodities to the civilian populations in spite of the diversion of industry and transport for war purposes, and to organize an efficient production of munitions to sustain the fighting fronts. For these ends it was indispensable to obtain the willing co-operation of the widest possible sectors of society and of public opinion in each country, including organized bodies representing both capital and labour – a situation which gave the latter a considerable bargaining leverage in pressing for social and political reforms. In Russia, where the bureaucracy proved incapable by itself of mobilizing the economic potential of the country for war, so-called War Industry Committees were set up with representatives of officialdom, industrialists and workers. This meant that the workers had an opportunity of playing a bigger part in public affairs than had ever previously been possible for them. But the Social Democrats, having refused any approval of the war effort, could not consistently nominate workers' representatives on the committees. Both the Bolsheviks and the Mensheviks' 'Secretariat in Exile' declined to take any part in their work. But a number of Mensheviks inside Russia, ignoring the decision of their leaders abroad, got themselves elected to the War Industry Committees and found they had, as a result, more influence with the workers than the Social Democratic Party had ever yet succeeded in obtaining.

Meanwhile, a conflict, aggravated by Russia's military defeats and very heavy casualties in the war, had developed between the Tsarist government on the one hand and the Duma and the War Industry Committees on the other. In the name of efficiency and of national solidarity in the prosecution of the war the parties of the Left in the Duma demanded a cabinet responsible to it, while the War Industry Committees claimed freedom to take measures for organizing the required increase of arms production. But the ruling bureaucracy was hostile to the intrusion of unofficial elements into the field of administration, while the Tsar was unwilling to concede any of his remaining autocratic powers which had not been given up in the Constitution of 1905. The domestic political situation was further complicated by the intrigues of the monk-adventurer Rasputin, who was believed by the Tsarina to possess God-given powers of healing; there is no evidence that he was a German agent, but he seriously disorganized the government at a critical time by using his influence to exclude from office able men who had incurred his dislike and to promote individuals of worthless character who had taken the trouble to court his favour. Among army officers it was rumoured that the Tsarina was secretly pro-German and that she was the mistress of Rasputin. In 1916 there was a military plot for the removal of Rasputin and the deposition of Nicholas II, but it had not yet resulted in any actual *coup d'état* when in November Rasputin was murdered by a group of members of aristocratic families including a close relative of the Tsar. If, after the elimination of Rasputin, Nicholas had been willing to appoint a Prime Minister who had the confidence of the Duma, he might have kept his throne. But he refused to make any concession to the rising demand for full parliamentary government, and forces more popular than the killers of Rasputin now began to take a hand in the dispute. In December 1916 the workers' sections of the local War Industries Committees formed a Central Workers' Group which demanded the immediate establishment of political democracy and mass action of the workers to attain this end. On 12 February 1917 the members of the Central Workers' Group were arrested by the police, but not before they had issued a call for street demonstrations in Petrograd – as St Petersburg had been renamed in response to patriotic and anti-German feeling since the outbreak of war – to coincide with the reassembly of the Duma on 27 February. On that day the workers did not go into the streets, but more than 100,000 went on strike and, during the next fortnight, with an aggravation of disturbances due to a breakdown of the food-rationing system, there were further strikes culminating in a mass invasion of the central area of Petrograd from the industrial suburbs. When the police proved inadequate to cope with the crowds and when soldiers of the Petrograd garrison refused to fire on them, a revolution took place. The authority of the Tsar had collapsed in his own capital, but he himself was at the front having taken over the supreme command of the army after the military reverses of 1915. He consulted his generals, who advised him to abdicate, and this he did on behalf of both himself and his son, transferring the inheritance of the dynasty to his brother the Grand Duke Michael. Neither Nicholas II nor the generals supposed that they were agreeing to the abolition of the monarchy. There had been no general uprising in the country and the army in the field was still under effective discipline. But the

President of the Duma, Rodzianko, a man of extremely nervous temperament, was seized with panic at the lawless behaviour of the Petrograd garrison, among whom republican sentiments were now being expressed, and persuaded the Grand Duke to abdicate as well. After centuries of dynastic autocracy, Russia was suddenly left without a monarch. A Provisional Government was set without a monarch. A Provisional Government was set up by the Duma, but the authority of the Duma itself was now undermined; having been elected on a restrictive franchise it could not claim to represent the whole people. A democratically legitimate government could only come into existence when new elections had been held on a basis of universal franchise, but this could not be done at once, for new electoral registers had to be prepared.

Meanwhile, a political vacuum had been created which the new Provisional Government was quite unable to fill. Composed of liberal politicians of the Duma – which proceeded to dissolve itself, transferring its powers to the democratic Constituent Assembly due to meet in the autumn – the new government found itself confronted with a revival of the Petrograd workers' council or soviet, which had been set up in the abortive revolution of 1905. Similar councils were set up in other cities, and delegates of rank-and-file conscript soldiers of the army – who were mostly of peasant origin – were added. The soviets did not yet claim exclusive possession of the state power, but they were dominated by the political parties of the extreme Left – Social Revolutionaries, Mensheviks and Bolsheviks, with the Bolsheviks at the outset in a small minority – and were not inclined to take orders from a government formed by the parties of the bourgeoisie. Moreover, in their first flush of ultra-democratic enthusiasm after the collapse of the Tsardom, and in their fear lest generals and army officers might attempt to restore it, they did not hesitate to undermine the discipline of the army which faced the German enemy on the field of battle and which was in the last resort the only instrument of power for holding together an imperial state in which the Russians themselves were only half the total population. On 1 March, even before the Tsar had abdicated, the famous Order No. 1 was issued in the name of the Petrograd Soviet to the garrison troops of Petrograd; it laid down that the rank and file of all military and naval units should elect committees which should take control of all weapons without regard to officers' commands, and that orders coming from the Military Commission of the Duma were only to be carried out if they were in harmony with the decisions of the Soviet of Workers' and Soldiers' Deputies. The Provisional Government was thus in effect excluded from control of the army, and the officers who remained with their units – many had been killed or driven out during the mutiny – were subject to a suspicious supervision by their own men. The system of soldiers' committees, first devised for the garrison troops in Petrograd, was soon extended to the army at the front, with the result that when in July the Provisional Government attempted to launch an offensive against the Germans in Galicia, the front there collapsed in uncontrollable confusion.

It was thus to a Russia wherein the authority of the state was in process of disintegration that Lenin returned in April 1917, having accepted the offer of the German government to provide him and a number of his fellow-exiles with railway transport through Germany. The purpose of the German General Staff in authorizing this conveyance was to promote in Russia the activity of a disruptive and anti-belligerent political force, which, if successful, could be expected to take Russia out of the war, and enable Germany to concentrate all her military strength on the Western Front. Needless to say, Hindenburg and Ludendorff had no sympathy for the aims of Lenin, nor had Lenin any intention of forwarding the purposes of Hohenzollern Germany, but both of them for very different reasons wanted a violent overturn of the Russian state. Both sought to use the other and both hoped in the end to destroy the other, for Lenin believed that a proletarian revolution victorious in Russia would spread to Germany, and the German High Command believed that if it could win the war on the Western Front, it would have little difficulty afterwards in disposing, with disciplined German troops, of the mobs of mutinous soldiers and armed workers who might take power in Russia.

When Lenin got back to Russia he found himself at odds, not only with the Social Revolutionaries and Mensheviks, but also with many leading members of his own Bolshevik faction. Lenin was determined not to co-operate in any way with the Provisional Government and not to support in any way a continuation of the war. But now that a political democracy had been achieved and that the soviets were in effect sharing in the state power, there was a general disposition among Russian Socialists to reach some kind of compromise with the liberals, if only to form a common front against the danger of monarchist counter-revolution, and to take some responsibility for carrying on the war, if only to keep the Germans out of the new democratic Russia. Against this tendency Lenin fought with all the polemical skill of which he was capable; its outcome, as he saw it, would be to consolidate and stabilize the bourgeois republic with a reorganized army, which, even if its leadership did not hanker after a restoration of the Tsardom, would be an insuperable barrier to a proletarian revolution. Lenin perceived the opportunity for a Bolshevik seizure of power in the disintegration of the army and the state which was going on in front of his eyes. He did not want to stop it, but to intensify it, and for this purpose he sought to devise a propaganda which would draw the masses to his side and stimulate them to a new disorderly upheaval. He found two suitable twin slogans in 'peace' and 'land'. The former meant that the Bolsheviks would end the war whether Russia's allies joined in the peace-making or not, and the latter meant that the peasants should seize and divide up the landlords' estates without delay, unilaterally ending their service in the army, if they were in it, for the purpose of taking part in the agrarian revolution. The non-Leninists in the soviets were all for ending the war and dividing up the land, but they wanted to keep the army in being for national defence and to carry out land reform through orderly administrative procedures. Neither the Social Revolutionaries nor the Mensheviks wanted a second revolution; the former, as the party of the peasants, were confident of getting a clear majority of votes in the coming elections to the Constituent Assembly, and the latter, as good Marxists, did not believe that the objective conditions were sufficiently developed in Russia for a proletarian seizure of power immediately after completion of the bourgeois-democratic revolution. Many of the Bolsheviks themselves, while more hostile than the Mensheviks towards the Provisional Government, thought that an attempt to take over the state power by force would have no prospect of success.

To provide a quasi-constitutional cover for his plans Lenin coined the slogan of 'all power to the soviets'. Since these were bodies composed of representatives of the working class, it would be a proletarian revolution if they were to take over the full authority of the state from the Provisional Government. The difficulty was that they were led by men who did not want to take over the full powers and responsibilities, and even if they did, it would not be to Lenin's liking if the government were to be in the hands of Social Revolutionaries and Mensheviks. What he wanted was power for his own party, not for anyone else. The aim of the slogan was to expose the non-Bolshevik leaders in the eyes of the more militant workers as cowards and turncoats who were afraid to seize on behalf of the proletariat the power which might be theirs. Lenin's first move, however, was a failure and nearly ruined the Party's prospects. The Party organized a mass street demonstration in Petrograd in July on the occasion of the First Congress of Soviets, to be attended by delegates of local soviets all over Russia; the demonstration was banned by the Provisional Government with the concurrence of the Petrograd Soviet, and when it nevertheless took place the crowd was dispersed with rifle fire. An order was issued for Lenin's arrest and he went into hiding. But the situation soon afterwards turned in favour of the Bolsheviks. The Provisional Government, now headed by a 'Trudovik' Socialist, Kerensky, had appointed as Commander-in-Chief of the Army a general of peasant origin named Kornilov. Kornilov declared that he could not take responsibility for holding the front against the Germans unless measures were taken to restore discipline in the army and curb the powers of the soldiers' committees. At first Kerensky agreed to his proposals, but then became suspicious of his intentions and denounced him as a counter-revolutionary; Kornilov tried to move troops to Petrograd, but they would not follow him and he was arrested.

The supposed threat of a military dictatorship rallied all the parties of the Left in defence of the democratic republic, and in this cause the Bolsheviks had the opportunity to arm their paramilitary groups of factory workers known as Red Guards. In new elections they gained a majority in the Petrograd Soviet, which could henceforth be used to endorse their actions. A Second Congress of Soviets was due to be convened in the capital early in November and the nation-wide universal-franchise elections for the Constituent Assembly were to be held later in the same month. Lenin resolved to anticipate both events. At a meeting of the Bolshevik Party Central Committee on 23 October it was decided that 'an armed rising is inevitable and the time is perfectly ripe'. Lenin did not get his way at this meeting without a struggle. Both Zinoviev and Kamenev opposed the proposal to stake the fortunes of the Party on an immediate seizure of power. Lenin, however, was supported by Trotsky, who after having long pursued an independent political course between the Bolsheviks and the Mensheviks had at last joined the former and had been elected to their Central Committee. Trotsky could indeed claim that he had converted Lenin to his views rather than become himself a convert, for the idea that a socialist revolution could and should follow immediately on a bourgeois-democratic one had originally been his rather than Lenin's. But both men were now at one in the intention to seize power as soon as possible, and while Lenin remained in hiding – since the Government's order for his arrest had not been withdrawn – Trotsky took charge of the actual preparations for the *coup d'état*. A Military Revolutionary Committee was set up in the name of the Petrograd Soviet and assumed control of the troops in the city. The only force in the capital on which the Provisional Government could now rely consisted of a detachment of officer cadets which was stationed to guard the seat of the government in the Winter Palace. The insurrection took place on 7 November; the Winter Palace was captured after brief fighting and most of the Ministers were arrested. Kerensky escaped and tried to rally some troops outside the city, but the officers, although they were anti-Bolsheviks, bitterly reproached him for his treatment of Kornilov and would not support him; he finally fled abroad.

When the Second Congress of Soviets met it was presented with a new government of Russia, styled a Council of People's Commissars, with Lenin as its 'Chairman'. It was at first a purely Bolshevik body, though later in one of his cleverest tactical manoeuvres Lenin succeeded in forming a political alliance with a breakaway Left faction of the loosely organized Social Revolutionary Party, and a few portfolios in the new government were assigned to this group. In effect the Bolsheviks were now in power. Their *fait accompli* was endorsed by the Congress of Soviets which provided the new government with a revolutionary legitimacy as representative of the Russian proletariat. But Lenin did not intend to make his authority in future depend on the approval of a freely elected Congress of Soviets. It was the Party which was going to govern and the Party would 'make' the elections.

Amid the enthusiasm which greeted the new regime at the Congress of Soviets after the overthrow of Kerensky's government an old man was brought to the platform. He was a veteran of the Paris Commune of 1871. Symbolically the proletarian revolution of Russia affirmed its inheritance of the revolutionary tradition of France. But in 1871 France had not followed Paris, and the Commune had been suppressed by forces entering the capital from outside. In 1917 it remained to be seen whether Russia would follow Petrograd.

6. Foreign Intervention and Civil War

When Lenin and the Bolshevik Party became the government of Russia in November 1917 they took over the authority of a state in which the civil administration had already been seriously disorganized by revolution, the economy was strained by the maintenance of a huge army in the field against a most formidable external enemy, and the army itself was already disintegrating owing to the breakdown of discipline and the antagonism between officers and men. The *coup d'état* of 7 November did not so much establish a new central government in Russia as accelerate the forces of disruption which were rendering any orderly administration impossible.

The first problem was what to do about the war. In his first speech to the Congress of Soviets as head of the new government Lenin declared:

We shall offer peace to the peoples of all the belligerent countries upon the basis of the Soviet terms – no annexations, no indemnities, and the right of self-determination of peoples. At the same time, in accordance with our promises, we shall publish and repudiate all secret treaties.... This proposal of peace will meet with resistance on the part of the imperialist governments; we don't fool ourselves on that score. But we hope that revolution will break out in all the belligerent countries.... If the German proletariat realizes that we are ready to consider all offers of peace, revolution will break out in Germany.

There can be little doubt that Lenin believed what he said; he was really confident that all Europe was ripe for proletarian revolution and that after the vast slaughter of three years of war the masses of the people everywhere would respond at once to the Bolsheviks' appeal and insist on the immediate cessation of hostilities. He does not seem to have considered seriously the possibility that the war might go on and that the effect of the Bolshevik initiative might be that Russia would have to conclude a separate peace with Germany in a situation of total military defeat. If the Bolshevik appeal did not produce the expected result in other belligerent countries Russia would need at least to keep her army in being so that Germany would not be able to dictate terms. But the Bolshevik Revolution completed the disintegration of the Russian army which was already far advanced. For months Bolshevik agitators had been telling the soldiers that the Tsar's government had involved the country in war for the sake of sordid capitalist interests, that the officers of the army were their class enemies, and that they could have peace at once if only Kerensky and his friends were driven from power. Now there was a Bolshevik government and it offered the Germans an armistice, which was accepted. The soldiers naturally concluded that the war was over, and they started off for their homes in tens of thousands without waiting to be demobilized; they commandeered trains and usually took their rifles with them, but left their artillery and heavy equipment behind. The Bolsheviks could not have stopped this elemental mass movement even if they had wanted to; officers who tried to stop it were killed or driven away and the Chief of the General Staff, General Dukhonin, was torn to pieces on the platform of the railway station at Mogilev. Within three months of the Bolshevik seizure of power Russia no longer possessed an organized army; there were only the Red Guards in the cities and soldier-peasant bands in the countryside engaged in taking over and looting the mansions of the former landowning gentry.

Lenin nevertheless hoped that in peace negotiations with the Germans a high-powered political propaganda could make up for Russia's vanishing military power. There had been no response to the Soviet peace appeal from the British or French governments nor had the British or French peoples risen in revolt; Russia's allies, at both official and popular levels of opinion, regarded the action of the new Russian government as a betrayal of the common cause and were inclined to give credence to the accusation that Lenin was a German agent. Germany on the other hand was only too willing to conclude a separate peace with Russia in order to eliminate the Eastern Front and concentrate German forces against Britain and France, now about to be reinforced by United States troops from the other side of the Atlantic. But the Germans wanted peace with Russia on terms corresponding to the military success they had already achieved by overrunning a large area of Russian territory and capturing Warsaw, Vilna and Riga. They demanded the separation from Russia of Poland, Lithuania and Courland, which were to become nominally independent states (in accordance with the Bolsheviks' advocacy of the 'self-determination of peoples'), but would be in fact German protectorates.

At Brest-Litovsk Russian Bolshevik and German delegates met to conclude a peace treaty. In order to emphasize the popular character of the new regime in Russia, in contrast to the upper-class representatives of the German Foreign Ministry and General Staff, the Bolshevik government included in its delegation an uneducated factory worker and an extremely uncouth peasant, but the actual negotiation was carried on by very sophisticated members of the Bolshevik intelligentsia—Trotsky, Joffe, Kamenev and Sokolnikov. They played their diplomatic cards with considerable skill, but in the end they were faced with the hard choice between acceptance of the German terms and renewal of the war. Well publicized speeches with rhetorical appeals to the German and Austrian peoples had proved of no avail; the German and Austrian peoples did nothing to remove their governments, and the Soviet delegates continued to be faced at Brest-Litovsk with the implacable Colonel Hoffman representing the hard line of German Eastern policy. Meanwhile, as part of the disintegration of Russia, the Ukraine had declared itself an independent state and Germany concluded a separate peace treaty with it to the great embarrassment of the Russians.

In Russia news of the German peace terms produced a widespread patriotic indignation potentially dangerous to any government which accepted them. Among the Bolsheviks themselves there were many advocates of a 'revolutionary war' against Germany as an alternative to a German-dictated peace. Lenin, however, disillusioned by now about the German revolution, did not believe that Russia could fight Germany without an army. At Brest-Litovsk Trotsky refused to accept the German terms and proclaimed a state of 'neither peace nor war'. The Germans then denounced the armistice and their army moved forward into Russia as fast as its transport could keep up with it; there was nobody to oppose them and there was nothing to stop them from advancing to Petrograd and Moscow. Lenin persuaded the Central Committee to bow to *force majeure* and the peace treaty of Brest-Litovsk was signed on 3 March 1918.

By drastic cessions of territory, renouncing all Russian claims to former Russian Poland, the Ukraine, the Baltic Provinces and Finland, Russia had bought peace with Germany. But the Soviet government had now to deal with Russia's former allies. Its policy had done nothing to conciliate the nations from whose camp Russia had withdrawn in order to make a separate peace with Germany. Its decrees of expropriation of capitalist property had not spared foreign any more than Russian enterprises, and substantial British and French capital investments had been taken over. On 10 February the Soviet government repudiated all Russia's external debts incurred before the Bolshevik Revolution, amounting to fourteen milliards of roubles, of which twelve milliards were owed to the Allied and Associated Powers, mostly to France. Thus there were large numbers of company shareholders and bondholders in Britain and France who had a strong interest in the removal of the Bolshevik regime quite apart from the general disapproval of such a regime to be expected from the bourgeoisie of all countries. But it is unlikely that there would have been any actual military intervention in Russia but for the war situation and the fear that large stocks of arms which had been sent to Russia to equip the Russian army in its fight against Germany might be seized by the Germans or handed over to them. These arms were for the most part still stored at Murmansk and Archangel and Allied expeditions were sent to both places to recover them, though in rather different circumstances at each place, for whereas the move to Archangel was a definitely anti-Bolshevik one, that to Murmansk was directed against German troops who had been sent to Finland to assist the anti-Bolshevik Finns, and the landing of Allied troops was at the invitation of the local Soviet.

Meanwhile, events which had occurred in the interior of Russia drew the Allies into a further involvement in Russian affairs. When the Russian army dissolved itself there was one military force which remained intact; this was the Czech Legion formed from Austrian prisoners of war or deserters of Czech nationality who had volunteered to fight on the Russian side for the creation of an independent Czech state as part of Allied war aims. When Russia withdrew from the war, the Czechs had no reason for remaining in Russia and conceived the project of going eastward across Siberia to Vladivostok and getting American ships to take them to France, where they could fight on the Western Front. The Soviet government, however, having become a neutral in relation to the European war, was not disposed to assist in the project, and there were clashes between the Czechs and local authorities, as a result of which the Czechs seized several strategic points on the Trans-Siberian railway. The Allied Powers decided to intervene to help the Czechs get out of Russia and encouraged Japan to land troops at Vladivostok for the purpose. But this intervention soon involved support for anti-Bolshevik Russian forces, for the Russo–Czech conflict had in the summer of 1918 got mixed up with a Russian civil war.

The Bolsheviks did not meet with any serious armed opposition during the six months that followed their seizure of power in Petrograd and Moscow. The former propertied classes were naturally hostile to the revolution, but their political parties were dissolved and they were intimidated by the Red Guards and anti-bourgeois mobs. The regular army had ceased to exist and those of its officers who had survived the mutinies were scattered over the country without leadership or cohesion. The peasants were busy seizing and dividing the estates of the landlords and hardly noticed it when the Constituent Assembly in which their representatives were in a majority was forcibly dissolved by the Bolsheviks. The elections were held after the Bolsheviks came to power, and the parties of the Right were in effect prevented from taking part in them, but the Bolsheviks did not have time to rig them in the countryside, and peasant votes, as anticipated, gave the Social Revolutionary Party a comfortable majority of seats in the Assembly. Of 707 deputies elected 370 were Social Revolutionaries, 175 Bolsheviks, 40 Left Social Revolutionaries (the splinter group allied with the Bolsheviks), 17 *Kadety* (Constitutional Democrats, a liberal party) and 16 Mensheviks.[1] Such a body was unacceptable to the Bolsheviks and after it had shown itself recalcitrant to their dictation on the first day of its meeting (18 January 1918) they dissolved it by force. They now proclaimed that not the Constituent Assembly, but the Congress of Soviets, was to be recognized by them as the sovereign legislature of the Russian people. This was an assembly which could be manipulated much more easily than one elected by direct, equal and universal franchise. The soviets had originally represented only

1. Leonard Schapiro, *The Communist Party of the Soviet Union*, p. 183.

workers and soldiers (who might be of either rural or urban origin); later peasant soviets were also set up, but they were combined with the urban ones on the principle that five peasant votes were equivalent to one working-class vote – a rule designed to ensure working-class preponderance in a 'democratic dictatorship of workers and peasants'. Moreover, the soviets had been improvised political bodies elected at mass meetings without any regular electoral procedure, and the central Congress consisted of delegates elected by the soviets; it was not difficult for the Bolsheviks with their tight party organization to order and rig these elections in such a way as to obtain the results required. The Constituent Assembly elections indicated that in the period after their seizure of power the Bolsheviks could count on a majority of urban working-class votes, but that the majority of the peasants (who were over three quarters of the population) favoured the Social Revolutionary Party. In the Soviet Congress system the Social Revolutionary majority was nullified. If the peasants accepted this more easily than might have been expected, it was because their main preoccupation was with the redivision of the land, and the Bolsheviks were at any rate providing a strong government unalterably opposed to any return of the landlords.

The Bolsheviks, however, were not content to rely merely on votes even with the aid of electoral manipulation. They saw from the outset that a special instrument of force was needed if their precarious party dictatorship was to be consolidated. Before the seizure of power Lenin had called in phrases of a revolutionary romanticism for 'abolition' of the army and police as professional bodies and direct performance of the coercive functions of the state by the 'armed people'. The hated Tsarist police had in fact been replaced by a militia and the regular army by the Red Guards, who were simply armed factory workers. But something more specialized and more closely controlled by the Bolshevik Party was required to combat the potential enemies of the Revolution, who were now deemed to include not only promoters of a Tsarist restoration, but also liberal democrats and non-Bolshevik socialists. The Soviet government from the outset took power to censor or suppress newspapers and used it rigorously. Further, on 20 December 1917, after it had been in power only six weeks, it set up an Extraordinary Commission for the suppression of Counter-revolution, Speculation and Sabotage, which quickly developed into a powerful secret police force with its own prisons and its own armed detachments for crushing resistance and making arrests. From a contraction of its Russian title this body came to be known as the Cheka, and through several changes of name, as G P U, N K V D, M V D and K G B, it has remained ever since a permanent feature of the Soviet regime.

A new police force was followed by a new army. The amateur Red Guards were replaced by the Red Army. It was formed on a class basis as an instrument of proletarian power. There was no lack of men for it, but the difficulty was to find officers. They were obtained from three sources: officers of the former regular army who had joined the Bolsheviks; non-commissioned officers of the old army; and Bolshevik Party members who were specially trained for the purpose. It took time to get the Red Army organized and it was not an effective fighting force until 1919.

Opposition to Bolshevik rule came from three different quarters. There were firstly the politicians of the democratic parties, including the Mensheviks, the Social Revolutionaries and the *Kadety*, who had welcomed the March Revolution, but had been deprived of its fruits by the Bolsheviks; they wanted a democratic republic with free elections and an agrarian settlement which would give the land to those who cultivated it. Secondly there were the national separatists of Poland, Lithuania, Latvia, Estonia, Finland, Byelorussia, the Ukraine, Georgia, Armenia, Azerbaijan, Turkestan and other non-Russian areas of what had been the Russia of 1914; they wanted national independence for their respective countries, incidentally thus depriving the residual Russia of the former Russia's main resources of grain, coal, iron and oil. Thirdly there were the ex-officers of the former Russian army, who came mostly from the landed gentry and had been brought up to believe in God, Russia and the Tsar; they were in general hostile to both democracy and national separatism and unwilling to accept the complete loss of their estates. All these factors of opposition added up to a formidable total if they could be combined, but, as events were to show, they could not be combined effectively; the unified and disciplined strength of the Bolsheviks was confronted with an opposition whose power was nullified by its internal dissensions and contradictions.

Apart from a brief resistance of the Don Cossacks under General Kaledin in the period immediately after the Bolshevik Revolution, the first considerable military force to take the field against the Soviet regime was that formed by a group of generals in the western Caucasus early in 1918; it attracted numbers of ex-officers, who made their way from various parts of Russia to join it, and it achieved a series of successes over local Red Guards and Soviet levies. It was originally commanded by Kornilov, who in December 1917 had escaped from the prison where he had been confined since his arrest in September, but he was killed in action in March 1918, and succeeded by Denikin, under whom further ground was gained. Then in the summer of 1918 the defeat of Soviet forces by the Czech Legion enabled anti-Bolshevik Russian forces to emerge in Siberia and the region of the middle Volga; they came under the leadership of Admiral Kolchak, a former officer of the Black Sea Fleet. Another White army came into being with the support of the British expeditionary force in Archangel. A fourth, which only became operative after the defeat of Germany, was built up in the German occupation zone in the Baltic Provinces; it was later commanded by General Yudenitch.

Until November 1918 the Ukraine was an independent state with a government supported by a German occupation army, but after Germany's defeat on the Western Front and the withdrawal of all German military forces from Russia, as required by the terms of the Armistice, both Red Russian and White Russian forces invaded the Ukraine and engaged in fighting both with each other and with Ukrainian nationalists. Denikin showed himself a capable military commander, but an incompetent political leader; he was unwilling to make concessions either to the peasants in the vital matter of agrarian reform or to the Ukrainian nationalists, whereas the Bolsheviks not only defended the peasants' claims to the lands they had seized, but also promised the Ukrainians autonomy in a federal union with Russia. Denikin reached a point only 200 miles south of Moscow, but was then defeated; the other White armies, whose operations had never been properly co-ordinated with Denikin's, also suffered defeat in detail. In 1920 the Russian civil war was complicated by the intervention of the new independent state of Poland which gave support to the Ukrainian nationalists led by Petlura. In a campaign which saw extraordinary vicissitudes of fortune the Poles were successful in driving back the Soviet Russian army which nearly captured Warsaw, but Petlura was forced to leave the Ukraine, and Denikin's army which had withdrawn to the Crimea – Denikin having been replaced in its command by General Wrangel – was evacuated by sea to Turkey, where it was interned, in the autumn of 1920.

The White armies came very near to overthrowing the Bolshevik government in the summer of 1919. Their final collapse involved in a common ruin everyone who had been opposed to the Bolsheviks from Social Revolutionaries to the most extreme conservatives. Because the former regular army officers were the only people who could provide military organization they became politically dominant on the side of the Whites and thwarted politicians such as Chernov and Krivoshein who might have won decisive mass support for their cause. A majority of the Russian people were in fact in the middle of the road, as the Constituent Assembly voting had showed, and many Russians described themselves as *ninisti* or 'Neithers', meaning that they supported 'neither Lenin nor Kolchak'. But in the circumstances of the civil war one had to be either for Lenin or for Kolchak. Confronted with this choice, the bulk of the peasantry chose Lenin; they were determined to keep the land they had taken. They deserted wholesale when conscripted for the White armies and formed guerrilla bands which disrupted their communications. They tilted the balance of the civil war and decided it in favour of a proletarian revolution, in contrast to the France of 1848 and 1871, when a peasantry endowed with property by the original French Revolution had formed part of the conservative opposition to the insurrections of the Parisian proletariat.

The foreign support given to the Whites probably did them more harm than good. The Czech Legion gave them valuable initial help, and supplies of arms from abroad gave them equipment which they would otherwise have lacked. But the direct military assistance of Britain, France and Japan to the White armies was very small, and it was more than offset by the political opportunity it gave to the Bolsheviks to appeal to Russian patriotic sentiment. The Bolsheviks had not been able to do this when they were working for the disintegration of the Russian army or when they were negotiating a disastrous separate peace with Germany. But after Germany had gone down in defeat, Bolshevik Russia stood alone and the regime could not be suspected of serving a foreign power; it was now the turn of the Whites to incur the charge of selling their country to foreigners. The idea that the Bolsheviks at least stood for an independent Russia had a marked effect on many Russians whose class interests and sympathies were certainly not with the proletarian revolution; this was so particularly after the entry of the Poles into the conflict, when many ex-officers, moved by the age-long Russian antipathy towards Poland, volunteered for service in the Red Army.

One thing would almost certainly have smashed the Soviet regime – a decisive German military victory over the Allies on the Western Front in 1918. If that had happened, as it very nearly did, there can be no doubt but that the German army would afterwards have been used to restore the Tsardom in Russia. The rulers of Germany in 1917 had been ready for strategic reasons to assist the Bolsheviks in their task of destroying the Russian state, but their basic attitude was one of profound hostility to a cause diametrically opposed to everything for which they stood. Once victorious in the West, they would have struck against the new revolutionary power in the East, and struck with all their might, using not small seaborne expeditions to remote sea-ports on the periphery of Russia, but an army which already held Narva, Pskov, Mogilev and Kharkov as bases for attack. It is very unlikely that the new-born Red Army would have been able to withstand such an onslaught. The Soviet regime, however, was saved from it by the Allied victories on the Western Front and an Armistice which imposed on Germany an obligation to withdraw all troops from Russia and the Ukraine. Fortunately for Lenin the Allied governments did not consider their class interests, but only their national war aims, or they would not thus have destroyed German power to the advantage of their common anti-capitalist enemy.

7. The Comintern

Lenin's antagonism to the Mensheviks within the Russian Social Democratic Party inevitably led to a similar attitude towards Socialists of a comparable type in the labour movements of other countries. When in 1914 the official Social Democrat, Socialist and Labour parties in Germany, France and Britain gave their support to the war efforts of their respective countries, Lenin denounced this as a betrayal of the cause of the international working class and declared that a new international organization would have to be created to replace the one which had been disrupted by the loyalty of its member parties to belligerent nations ranged on opposite sides in the European war. But in the years from 1914 to 1917 it did not look as if Lenin would have much success in creating a new international. In spite of the years he spent in exile in Western Europe he had very few friends among Socialist politicians in Western countries, and at the conferences of anti-war Socialists from various countries which were held in neutral Switzerland, at Zimmerwald in 1915 and at Kienthal in 1916, he found most of the delegates opposed to his ideas. But after the Bolshevik capture of power in Russia in November 1917 there was inevitably throughout Europe a strong undercurrent of working-class sympathy and admiration for the new regime. If this was not at once exploited by Lenin in order to create a new international, it was because of the extreme difficulty of making political contacts during the war with like-minded political elements whether in Austria and Germany or in countries allied to Russia; every country at war imposed the strictest limitations on non-official travel and after Germany's help for Lenin's return to Russia no non-Bolshevik government was willing to facilitate the movements of revolutionary agitators. It was only after the war had come to an end that an international gathering of pro-Bolsheviks from various countries was a practical proposition, and even then delegates from outside Russia had great difficulty in reaching Moscow because of the Allied blockade and the civil war operations of the White Russian armies. The conference met in Moscow in March 1919 and set up the new organization, the Communist or Third International, later to be commonly known as the Comintern. At this first Congress, however, the representation was very uneven; France was represented only by two Frenchmen who were living in Russia, United States by John Reed, Britain and Italy not at all. The most important non-Russian figure at the Congress was the German Eberlein, and this was appropriate, for it was on a revolution in Germany that Bolshevik hopes were primarily set. It was true that the German proletariat had failed to rise a year previously when the German army had imposed on a self-disarmed Russia the Treaty of Brest-Litovsk. But now Germany was defeated, the Kaiser was in exile, and the German people were impoverished, embittered and disillusioned with the political order under which they had lived. Superficially there seemed to be a resemblance between the state of affairs in Germany in the months following the Armistice of November 1918 and that which had existed in Russia after March 1917. In both a previously strong military-monarchical power had collapsed and a new democratic political system had not yet been established; this was the situation which the Bolsheviks had used to snatch power in St Petersburg in 1917 and it seemed that the same thing might happen in Berlin in 1919. But there was one basic difference between Germany and Russia in the aftermath of the fall of their monarchies; although Germany had suffered military defeat, there was no general breakdown of military discipline such as had occurred in Russia in 1917 and had deprived the Provisional Government of the capacity to maintain order. Those German troops who were to be demobilized gave up their arms at the crossings of the Rhine and dispersed to their homes unarmed; the military formations which were allowed to remain under the terms of the Armistice obeyed the orders of their officers and could not be used for a proletarian revolution, but only against it. This was in fact what happened when the extreme break-away group of the German Social Democrats known as the *Spartakusbund* declared themselves a Communist Party and attempted to follow the Bolshevik example by raising an insurrection in the streets of Berlin in January 1919. A government of Social Democrats called in troops to crush the rising, and the 'Spartacist' leaders, Karl Liebknecht and Rosa Luxemburg, were murdered by a mob after being captured. By the time the Comintern was founded the prospects of Bolshevism in Germany had already faded.

But what really was the point in having an international organization at all? Why should not the revolutionary proletarian element in each country get on with trying to make its own revolution without bothering about what was happening elsewhere; the leaders in each country presumably knew the conditions in the land where they lived better than any foreigner could tell them and they were best qualified to decide when, where and how to act. To be sure, it might be a good idea to have from time to time international conferences at which leaders from various countries could meet for mutual encouragement and exchange of views. But in the Marxist conception of an International there had always been something more than this. Marxism was essentially international in outlook; it claimed to be a philosophy of universal application and regarded national boundaries as being of no importance. The national state belonged to the feudal and bourgeois classes; the politically conscious proletarian knew only his solidarity with

his fellow-workers all over the world, and for him therefore a world society transcending all territorial frontiers
already existed. A Socialist International, therefore,
should embody this universal solidarity of the workers,
and it was proper that it should not merely provide a
forum for talk but have an executive organ which could
guide and co-ordinate the activities of member parties
in the various constituent countries. This idea of an
International as a sort of world federation of working-
class parties certainly goes back to the early days of
Marxism, but it had never before 1919 produced an
authority which could really issue directives to the constituent national parties. By 1919, however, an entirely
new situation had arisen. A Socialist (renamed Communist) party in one country, namely Russia, had captured the state power in that country, whereas like-
minded parties or groups elsewhere were still outside the
gates of government. It was natural for the latter to
look up with awe and admiration to their Russian comrades and for the latter to take a great pride in their
achievement and set themselves up as tutors and guides
for the less successful (and presumably less competent)
revolutionaries of other lands. In this relation of attitudes
there was a basis for an International, which would not
be a mere federation of equal parties but a system of satellites under the leadership of one dominant party, the
Russian. The tendency for Communist parties formed
outside Russia to become mere vassals for the Russian
party was at the beginning a genuinely voluntary one,
due partly to their willingness to accept tutelage from
the Bolsheviks, whom they so much admired, and partly
to their hope of some day receiving help from Russia
for their own revolution in the form of money, arms
and perhaps military intervention. But once a central
organization had been set up with a permanent secretariat, the bonds by which the Soviet Communist Party,
the CPSU, could hold the others under its sway came to
be of a more compelling character. The central organiza-

tion had to be in Russia, for the country under Communist rule was naturally the only one which would give a home to an international body aiming at the violent overthrow of all non-Communist governments. But the fact that the central administration of the International was located permanently in Russia meant that its non-Russian staff were living under the jurisdiction of the Soviet Union and were subject to the same pressures and compulsions as any member of the C P S U. Moreover the leaders of the non-Russian communist parties could not be in two places at once; if they were in their own countries they could not take part in the day-to-day direction of the Comintern, and if they were more or less resident in Moscow they could not effectively manage the affairs of their own parties. Thus a system of centralized international control of the world Communist movement involved in practice a Russian direction of it.

This Russian-dominated character of the Comintern had three important consequences. It meant first of all a splitting of the labour movement in all countries. There had always been in this movement an inevitable divergence between moderate and extremist elements, between reformists and revolutionaries, between the less and the more militant. But in so far as there was a strong sense of common class interest in conflict with capitalism and bourgeois political parties, there was always the possibility of including the diverse trends within one loosely organized political party or at least of a genuine co-operation between different parties with a basically proletarian outlook. The advent of the Comintern changed this situation decisively. The Communist parties claimed to be the sole depositories of doctrinal truth and the sole legitimate representatives of the working class; all non-Communist socialist parties or groups were fakes, traitors, 'lackeys of capitalism'. The tight organization and discipline of the Communist parties, their fanatical intolerance, their bitter polemics and unscrupulous tactics in dealing with other working-class parties, far from unifying the world proletariat in a great struggle against capitalism, introduced an unprecedented disunity. The quarrel between Bolsheviks and Mensheviks was projected into the countries of the West; everyone had to be either for Lenin or against him. The leaders of the established Labour and Socialist parties in Western Europe refused to submit to the dictation of the new prophets and they were able to hold a large proportion of their followers, largest in Britain, where the labour movement had grown out of bourgeois radicalism and had been only slightly influenced by Marxism, and least in France, where *la mystique de la gauche* gave the new revolutionary doctrine a pervasive appeal. But everywhere Communist parties came into existence and were strong enough seriously to modify the alignments of left-wing politics as they had existed in 1914.

The second major consequence of the founding of the Comintern was that large numbers of people in Western Europe came to be deeply influenced by a way of thinking and acting which had its origin in the political conditions and experience of Russia. This was something for which there was no precedent. Russia had been regarded as backward and reactionary by both the bourgeois liberals and the socialists of Western Europe, certainly not as a source of enlightenment and inspiration. There had certainly been a widespread admiration for Russian literature and music and a susceptibility to *charme slave*, but nobody had thought of Russia as a model of social and political progress. With the foundation of the Comintern, however, the widespread working-class sympathy and admiration for the Soviet regime was, so to speak, institutionalized, so that everywhere in Western Europe there were enclaves of people who looked to Moscow for instruction and guidance. Russia had received Marxism from Western Europe, and Marxism was a doctrine developed in its increasingly democratic political environment. But now Western Europe was receiving

Leninism from Russia, and this was a doctrine developed in the authoritarian environment of Tsarist Russia and perpetuating in its elitist quasi-military type of party organization the ways of a society in which the penetration of liberalism had been late and ineffective. Thus Communism in Western Europe was a political force which was no less anti-democratic than anti-capitalist, and indeed its influence was far greater in undermining the ideology of political democracy than in making converts to socialist economics. As advocates of socialism the Communists were preaching to the converted; they gained their recruits almost entirely among people who were already socialists by conviction or inclined in that direction. But their scorn for constitutional parliamentary politics, their glorification of violence and their approval of unlimited dictatorial coercion in the creation of the new society at which they aimed had their influence in quarters which were not socialist at all. The Communist type of organization, its conception of party dictatorship and its technique of mass propaganda and agitation could be very easily adapted to purposes of quite a different kind. Indirectly Communism helped to produce Fascism and National Socialism. The unremitting attack on the values of 'bourgeois democracy' and the derision for all moral and humanitarian scruples which might obstruct the pursuit of power had the effect of weakening the resistance of democracy in the West to the new tyrannies of the Right which were far better able to seize the power of the state than the Communists were. In 1933, after fifteen years of Communist disdain for the Weimar Republic and vilification of the Social Democrats, it was not Thaelmann but Hitler who established himself in the Chancellory of the Reich.

A third consequence of the Russian mastery of the Comintern and the one which was the most important of all for international relations, was the subordination of the non-Russian Communist parties to the state interest of the Soviet Union as distinct from the revolutionary leadership of the CPSU. At first, indeed, it was hardly comprehensible to any Communist that there could be such a distinction. The Soviet state was a power subject to the exclusive control of a Communist party; it could have no interest in anything but the success of proletarian revolutions everywhere in the world. But what if these revolutions were not achieved? The Soviet Union had to carry on as a sovereign state in a system of sovereign states; it had a territory and frontiers; it had to seek diplomatic relations with other states and perhaps even in certain circumstances alliances with them. It could not afford to be isolated and alone in the international system, for that would involve the risk of another hostile coalition such as had been formed during the period of anti-Bolshevik intervention in Russia in 1918–20. But if Russia was to have close and friendly relations with any capitalist states, how was this to be reconciled with the business of promoting universal revolution? It might become necessary to damp down revolutionary activity instead of kindling it and even to turn a blind eye to the violent suppression of local Communists by a government with which the Soviet Union needed to be aligned for the sake of its foreign policy as a state. The dilemma arose first with Germany and then later on with France. For nearly a decade and a half the Soviet Union found it profitable to cultivate good relations with Germany, and particularly with the German army, as a counter to the *bloc* of France, Poland and the Little Entente which had the ascendancy in Europe in the period after the First World War. After Hitler had come to power in Germany and switched German policy on to an anti-Soviet course, Moscow moved towards an alliance with France. In both alignments, since the question of war was ultimately involved, the Soviet state needed close relations above all with the military authorities of the country concerned, but in both, these, even though nominally non-political, were in fact socially conservative and inclined politically to the Right; they were precisely the elements of the nation most hostile to any threat of a proletarian socialist revolution and most likely to be deterred from any commitment to a military alliance by Soviet support for Communist activity. They would collaborate with Russia only if they did not take the threat of revolution seriously. This condition was met in Germany, where the officers of the Reichswehr had taken the measure of the German Communists; they had shot them down in the streets of Berlin, and regarded them as mere riff-raff who could never capture the state power in Germany. Therefore the Reichswehr was in favour of close relations with the Soviet Union as a foreign state which was ready to train German officers in its territory in the use of arms forbidden to Germany by the Treaty of Versailles and might be an ally in a future war against France and Poland. But the Franco-Soviet pact of 1935 never developed into a real alliance because there was in the eyes of the French Right a revolutionary situation in France; there were the electoral victory of the Popular Front, the *expérience Blum,* the occupation of the factories by striking workers and the echoes of the Spanish civil war. In Germany in the 1920s it had been possible for the Soviet government to have it both ways, to have close relations with the Reichswehr while directing the German Communists through the Comintern; in France in 1936-9 it was not possible similarly to run with the hare and hunt with the hounds. The domestic successes of the Communists in France drove the Right towards appeasement of Hitler; for the *bien pensants* Russia was identified with people who seized factories in Clichy and murdered priests in Madrid.

In general, the notorious 'dual policy' of the Soviet Communist regime in simultaneously dealing with foreign governments through a Commissariat of Foreign Affairs and working for their overthrow through the Comintern was an obstacle to the effective conduct of Soviet diplomacy. Soviet diplomats argued that the

Comintern was an affair of the Communist Party which did not involve the Soviet government, but since it was well known that the CPSU controlled both the Soviet government and the Comintern, this kind of legal distinction could not be taken seriously. The existence of the Comintern inevitably caused a degree of tension in the relations between the Soviet Union and capitalist states which did not necessarily follow from the fact that the Soviet Union had a socialist economic system. Many European statesmen after the end of the civil war in Russia were ready to accept the new regime as a factor of political life and to enter into diplomatic relations with it in spite of its repudiation of Tsarist debts and confiscation of foreign investments. But it was difficult to have normal relations with a nation whose leaders openly discussed at political conferences how to bring about the destruction of governments to which they sent ambassadors. As long as the Comintern failed to accomplish anything, foreign governments could regard it as a mere nuisance which need not seriously impede the transaction of business with the Soviet Union as between one state and another, but whenever the Communists in Western countries showed signs of becoming more than tiresome gadflies the responsibility was naturally laid at Russia's door. The Comintern could only gain successes at the expense of Soviet diplomacy.

It did not as a matter of fact do anything in Europe to cause real alarm between 1923 and 1936. After the failure of the Spartacist rising at the beginning of 1919 there were further outbreaks of proletarian violence in Central Europe in the same year – the Munich Soviet and the Bela Kun regime in Hungary – but these were likewise defeated. There were minor risings in Germany in 1920 and 1921; then in 1923 the French occupation of the Ruhr and the galloping inflation of the German currency produced what could be regarded as a revolutionary situation. The German Communists by this time had built up a large party organization and there were many

German workers ready to take part in actions of a violent revolutionary character. But the German Communist leadership showed only confusion and indecision, from which it was not rescued by the superior wisdom which was supposedly available for the strategy of revolution at the headquarters of the Comintern. Stalin held that 'the German comrades should be held back rather than urged on', and counsels of prudence prevailed to the extent of preventing any real bid to seize power, but not to the extent of stopping an insurrection in Hamburg in which many lives were lost to no purpose. After the crisis of 1923 it was recognized in Moscow that the bourgeois order in Western Europe had been reconsolidated and that there was no immediate prospect of a revolution in any major country. For the next thirteen years the Communists continued to rule in Moscow, but they did not rule anywhere else in Europe; in the whole area from the Atlantic to the Dniester governmental power seemed to be far beyond their reach. Then suddenly and unexpectedly in July 1936 armed workers controlled the streets of Madrid and Barcelona, and for a while history in Spain went the way that in Marxist theory it ought to go.

8. The Retreat from Socialism

At the same session of the Congress of Soviets at which Lenin announced the formation of the Council of People's Commissars as the Government of Russia, he declared by way of a programme: 'We will now proceed to construct the socialist order.' He could hardly indeed have said anything else; it would have made no sense to his hearers if he had told them that he had seized power through armed insurrection with the aim of promoting the further development of Russian capitalism. The power of the state was now in the hands of Lenin and his associates in the leadership of the Bolshevik Party; what were they to do with it except to use it to expropriate the exploiting capitalists and take the means of production into public ownership? Yet only twelve years previously, in 1905, Lenin had denounced 'the absurd, semi-anarchist idea of an immediate fulfilment of our maximum programme' and had written: [1]

The degree of Russia's economic development – an objective condition – together with the degree of organization of the broad proletarian masses – a subjective condition indissolubly bound up with the former – renders impossible the total and immediate emancipation of the working class. Only ignorant people fail to see the bourgeois character of the democratic transformation going on at present. To wish to attain socialism by other ways, without passing through the stage of political democracy, is merely to arrive at ridiculous and reactionary conclusions, in the political as well as in the economic fields.

Was it then that the situation had altered so funda-

[1]. Lenin, 'Two Tactics of the Social Democracy in the Democratic Revolution', *Collected Works*, Vol. 8, pp. 40–41.

mentally since 1905 or had Lenin simply changed his mind? In view of the economic and political backwardness of Russia his earlier view was certainly better Marxism – and so was that of the Mensheviks in 1917, which was virtually identical with that of Lenin in 1905. Lenin had indeed changed his mind, but in his own estimation it was the situation which had changed, and in much more than the passage of a dozen years in the growth of Russia's industrial capitalism and the spread of labour organization. As Lenin saw it, capitalism, both in Russia and elsewhere, was ripe for a socialist takeover in a way that would have been impossible to foresee before 1914, because all the European nations at war, in order to mobilize their economic resources for the prolonged and costly armed struggle, had imposed controls and regulations which already seemed to have brought private capitalism under state direction. In September 1917 he wrote: [2]

Socialism is nothing else but the stage which follows immediately that of state capitalist monopoly. It is none other than the state capitalist monopoly placed at the service of the whole people and thereby ceasing to be a capitalist monopoly. There is no middle term between the two systems. Monopolies must lead to socialism. The war has increased their number, their role and their importance.... The dialectic of history is such that the war has enormously accelerated the transformation of capitalist monopolies into state monopolies and thereby brought the advent of socialism considerably nearer.

Once he had overcome his ideological scruples about the ripeness of the time for socialism in Russia, Lenin was ready to advance at full speed towards socialist objectives, and it was in this mood that he felt himself spiritually back in the 'glad confident morning' of the *Communist Manifesto*, before Marx himself, and even more Marxism since the death of Marx, had yielded to the doubts and hesitations born of disappointing experi-

2. Lenin, *Collected Works*, Vol. 14, p. 217.

ence. For nearly seventy years the vision of the glorious new society which had seemed close at hand at the beginning of 1848 had eluded the grasp of those who sought to attain it, and had seemed to recede into the far distance rather than to come nearer, but now suddenly it once more glittered in the forefront of the field of vision, needing only one resolute step forward in order to reach it. All that was required was that the Bolsheviks must make up their minds once and for all to part company with all those who declared in the name of Marxism that the time was not yet ripe. As he said on his return to Russia in April 1917, Bolsheviks must 'change their underwear, give up the name of Social Democrats, and in the place of the rotten Social Democracy create a new socialist organization: the Communist one'.

Now in November the time had come, and Lenin proceeded to 'construct the socialist order'. But four years later the vision had faded, and by 1921 he was harping like any Menshevik on the backwardness of Russia: [3]

Cast a glance at the map. North of Vologda, south-east of Rostov and Saratov, and north of Tomsk, you will see endless expanses which could contain dozens of large civilized states. These territories still remain in patriarchal, half wild, if not absolutely savage, conditions.... Everywhere, for hundreds of miles, primitive tracks separate, or rather isolate, the villages from the railway stations – that is, from contact with civilization, with capitalism, with large industries, with the big cities.... Is it to be imagined that under such conditions Russia can pass immediately to socialism?

But it was not Lenin's critics, but Lenin himself, who had imagined that under such conditions Russia could pass immediately to socialism. Lenin indeed recognized that his judgement had been at fault, though he was careful, by the use of the first person plural instead of the first person singular, to include his faithful followers with himself in his confession: [4]

3. Lenin, *Collected Works*, Vol. 26, p. 338.
4. Lenin, ibid., p. 333.

We went too far on the path of the nationalization of commerce and industry, and in the suppression of local trade. Was it a blunder? Yes, without question. In this respect we have committed obvious blunders and it would be criminal not to see and realize that we have overstepped the limit.... Capitalism will remain inevitable so long as we are unable to effect a direct transition from small industry to socialism. An attempt completely to suppress private trade – which amounts to capitalism – would be an absurdity because such a policy is economically unfeasible, and it would be suicide because a party which attempted it would be doomed to failure. It is not the growth of the petty bourgeoisie and the small capitalist that has to be feared, but the prolongation of famine, of misery, of the shortage of food.

Lenin talked like this in 1921 because he recognized that he was faced with an appalling economic and political crisis, and just as in the spring of 1918 he persuaded his party to agree to the signing of the Treaty of Brest-Litovsk so as to avoid an even greater disaster, so now he was persuading it to retreat from full socialism and make a compromise with private property in order to escape from an upheaval which might destroy the regime. What had happened was that the Bolsheviks in the months after their seizure of power had nationalized all Russia's industry, but it had not remained productive. The parasitic capitalists who had been extracting surplus value from the labour of the industrial workers had all been deprived of their property, and the surplus value should have been available to increase the wages of the workers and raise their standard of living, but somehow, when they tried to lay their hands on it, it was not there. During the period of the civil war the munitions industry had been kept going after a fashion to meet the current needs of the Red Army, but every other branch of industry had declined, and even after the civil war was over it was found impossible to revive them. The workers, nominally in possession of the means of production and victorious in battle over the former owners of industry, were nevertheless faced with conditions of the greatest hardship, with universal shortages both of food and of commodities of all kinds, and their only consolation for the disappointment of their hopes of material betterment under socialism was the fact that those members of the former upper and middle classes who had not emigrated or been killed were now even worse off than they were. Moreover, even the low standard of living which the urban workers had to endure in 1921 was only maintained by a ruthless coercion of the peasantry. Since the run-down industry of the cities could no longer produce goods in sufficient quantity for exchange with foodstuffs from the countryside, the inclination of the peasants was to revert to a self-contained village economy and produce only enough for their own requirements; having got rid of their landlords, they did not see why they should support unproductive townspeople who could not pay for what they ate. The Bolshevik government, in order to provide food for the towns, was therefore compelled to requisition grain from the peasants and to crush by force any resistance to these exactions. As long as the civil war lasted, both workers and peasants were generally willing to put up with the hardships and sacrifices which the struggle demanded; the country was in a state of siege, much of its territory was occupied by hostile forces, and military transport had a priority for its communications. But when in the autumn of 1920 Wrangel's army left the Crimea, the Bolsheviks were left in control of all the territory of Russia except for the separated western borderlands and the temporary 'Far Eastern Republic', and they were faced with demands from those who had supported them for at least a first instalment of the Utopia which they had promised. They had now to reckon no longer with the White counter-revolution or with German, British, French or Polish invaders, but with the massive discontent of those who had worked and fought for them since they took power. Local peasant revolts broke out in widely separated areas; lacking any central direction, they were soon crushed, but others followed, and there were signs of disaffection among the troops sent to suppress them; finally the garrison of Kronstadt, the fortress covering the sea approach to Petrograd, mutinied and the rising was only overcome with bitter fighting and heavy loss of life. For Lenin this was the red light; to avert an even greater upheaval, the economy must somehow be revived and the only way to do it was to appeal, at least at the lower levels of the economy, to the despised incentives of private gain and the discarded mechanism of the free market. This was to be the 'new economic policy' of which Lenin made himself the advocate, using all his powers of persuasion to lead the Party in a great retreat. Some excuse was, however, required to explain why the contrary policy had ever been adopted, and it was found in the theory of 'war communism'. The hopeful endeavour to 'construct the socialist order' was represented as having been really only a temporary expedient adopted in order to meet abnormal conditions of war and civil war; now that these conditions no longer prevailed it was no longer necessary. Lenin put the case thus: [5]

'War communism' consisted in taking from the peasants the surplus of their produce and sometimes even a part of what was necessary for their subsistence. We made requisitions in order to feed the army and the workers.... 'War communism' was necessitated by the war and by the ruin of the country. It has not been and could not be a policy answering to the economic needs of the proletariat. It was but a temporary measure.

It is historically untrue that the construction of the socialist order was undertaken by Lenin in 1917 simply as a 'temporary measure'. The nationalization of the banks, of industry, of foreign and internal trade, was decreed when the war with Germany was supposed to be over and before Denikin or Kolchak had appeared

5. Lenin, *On the Food Tax*, April 1921.

on the scene. On the other hand, it could fairly be argued that the civil war, with its disruption and devastation, had created impossible conditions for the success of an unprecedented economic experiment. The difficulty is even now, to estimate how far the collapse of the Russian economy in 1918 and 1919 was due to the effects of blockade and civil war and how far to the confusion induced by a reckless takeover of Russian industry by the Bolsheviks without any previous experience or detailed forethought on the problems likely to be encountered. Some clues as to the difficulties which would probably in any case have arisen in the initial drive for socialism in Soviet Russia are provided by a study of what happened in the second great socialist offensive from 1928 onwards. The second attempt had the advantage of complete freedom from internal or external warfare; by 1928 the whole of the territory of the Soviet Union was under firm central administrative control, and the Western capitalist countries, if not exactly friendly to the Soviet regime, were only too willing to sell to it capital goods in exchange for timber and oil. But the measure of success achieved by the First Five-year Plan was not due solely, or even mainly, to the more peaceful conditions; it was above all the result of having a plan formulated in terms of budgetary finance and expenditure. The Bolshevik planners of 1928, whatever their shortcomings, had behind them the experience of a decade of economic administration and proceeded on the assumption that investment in various sectors of the economy must be calculated in monetary values of a stable currency. The Bolsheviks of 1917, on the other hand, approached the problems of socialist production and distribution as Utopian amateurs; they simply assumed that with the transfer from private capitalist to public ownership industrial concerns would continue to function as they had done before and that the abolition of the mechanism of the market would make no difference to their operation. The outcome would almost certainly have been disastrous even if there had been no blockade, no Denikin and no Kolchak.

But Lenin's recognition in 1921 of the fact that the economy was *in extremis*, and that it was necessary to reach a compromise with the motives of private profit in order to revive it, did not lead him to admit that the Mensheviks had been right, much less to contemplate a return to a multi-party democratic system in which he would submit himself to the votes of a free electorate. On the contrary, he was ready to take the most severe measures against those who had correctly forecast the results of his policies. 'The Mensheviks and Social Revolutionaries,' he declared in a speech in April 1921, 'whether open or disguised as non-party men, deserve nothing but prison.' Even this, in his view, was being generous to them, for in the wake of the civil war monarchists, Octobrists and *Kadety* who had not managed to escape abroad could expect no other fate than death. The Bolsheviks, indeed, were not only determined to retain exclusive dictatorial power in their own hands, but were in a sense compelled to do so, for they had suppressed all other parties with such ruthless severity that it would have been highly dangerous for them to relinquish power even if they had been willing. Moreover, having so effectively broken up and destroyed all organized political groupings other than their own, they could claim that there really was no alternative to their own rule; to loosen their hold on the reins of power would only be to plunge Russia back into the chaos from which she had so painfully emerged.

The Communist Party continued to hold the power of the state and it continued also to hold what were called the 'commanding heights of the economy' – the banks, heavy industry and foreign trade. Lenin maintained that as long as those heights were held, the proletarian state could afford to tolerate a revival of private enterprise in small light industries and in the commerce of foodstuffs and consumer goods. The 'new economic

policy' of compromise with captitalism would be temporary, just as 'war communism' had been, and would
be followed, when the time was ripe, by a new socialist
offensive. It would be for the Party to decide when the
time was ripe; this could not be predicted in advance.
The Communist Party was like an army which had been
compelled to make a strategic withdrawal in order to
avoid annihilation; its commander-in-chief would order
it to move forward again when he deemed that the situation justified it. But this was a decision which Lenin
never had the occasion to make, for soon after the adoption of the new economic policy he had his first stroke; it
was followed by others, compelling him to withdraw
entirely from public affairs, and he died on 21 January
1924.

He left behind him a Party in which power was concentrated in the hands of a small ring of men who had
been his associates in the leadership since 1917, but in
which no single individual had the clear supremacy
which he had enjoyed as its original founder and its
leader in the capture of the state power. It was this Party
without Lenin which had to decide when to resume the
advance towards full socialism – and indeed in effect
whether to resume it at all, for although full socialism
was the ultimate goal which nobody questioned, those
who had come to believe from the experience of the years
1917–21 that Russia was objectively unready for it might
well regard the policy adopted in 1921 as setting the right
course for a whole historical epoch. It was inevitable
that the question of basic economic strategy in the struggle
against capitalism should give rise to acute controversy
within the Party and it was inevitable also that this
controversy should be mixed up with personal rivalries
between individuals aspiring to succeed to Lenin's position of supreme leadership. What was perhaps not inevitable, and what at any rate nobody foresaw in 1924, was
that the outcome of the factional struggle within the
Party would be to subject it to a ruthless personal

autocracy which would have no prophetic mandate from the writings of Marx and Engels but would recall the rule of the most tyrannical of the Tsars.

9. Stalin and the Revolution from Above

In December 1925, when the Soviet Communist Party held its Fourteenth Congress, a discerning political observer might well have held the opinion that both in Russia and in Europe as a whole the period of turmoil which had followed the First World War and the Russian Revolution had been succeeded by a new era of stability. Between the Soviet regime and the capitalist West there seemed to have developed a condition of what in later times was to be known as peaceful coexistence; each had come, however unwillingly, to accept the other as a political reality not to be quickly or easily overcome. The Bolsheviks had been victorious over the White Russian counter-revolution and the foreign intervention which had aided it; on the other hand, they had failed to subdue Poland in 1920, and after the fiasco of the abortive uprising in Germany in 1923 had ceased to think of the European revolution as being just around the corner. On the side of Western capitalism there had been a revival of production and trade after the painful adjustments of the immediate post-war period, and even in Germany there was a new economic growth after the end of the great inflation; the West, however, recognized that the Soviet system was now firmly established within the borders of Russia and had more or less written off Tsarist debts and pre-war investments in the Russian empire as a total loss. The *cordon sanitaire* from the Arctic Ocean to the Black Sea appeared to be effectively containing the infected organism of the Russian people without undue provocation of the men in the Kremlin, for, however much they might wish otherwise, the nations composing it were too weak to be a military threat to

Russia. Within Western Europe the Locarno Treaty seemed to mark a real reconciliation of the new democratic Germany with France and Britain and point to a peaceful future with a gradual relaxation to the tensions and resentments arising out of the Treaty of Versailles.

Within Russia likewise it looked as if the great revolutionary storm was over and society had settled down to a new equilibrium which would endure for a long time. As a result of the introduction of the NEP (new economic policy) in 1921 Russia now had a mixed economy in which the banks and heavy industry were state-owned, but small-scale light industry was again in capitalist hands and agriculture was carried on by peasant smallholders paying a grain tax to the state but also selling their produce on the open market. All political power remained in the hands of the Communist Party, avowedly representing the class interest of the property-less proletariat, but for the sake of reviving production the Party had made certain concessions to private enterprise, which meant, in as much as the peasants were still approximately three quarters of the total population, that the bulk of the inhabitants of Russia – now transformed into a Union of Socialist Soviet Republics – continued to have a stake in a system of private property in the means of production. This was certainly far from being a harmonious society, but it represented a balance of real social forces which ensured at least a relative stability after the chaotic violence of the civil war period. It was, broadly speaking, satisfactory to the peasants because as a result of the expropriation of the landlords' estates they had more land than before the war and were now able to make a profit out of it. It was considered to be a satisfactory solution by the right wing of the Communist Party because, even though it had involved a retreat from full socialism, it still left the way open for a gradual advance towards the socialist goal. According to Bukharin, the most eminent theorist of the NEP, the prosperity of peasant agriculture would not only assure a sufficient supply of food to the towns and of industrial raw materials such as cotton, wool and leather; it would also through taxation provide funds for the expansion of industry and by its purchasing power create a market for industrial goods. Thus industry would grow and with it the numbers of the industrial proletariat; meanwhile the peasants could be educated to see the benefits of co-operation in agriculture and of mechanized farming, when sufficient machinery would be available, and would thus gradually and painlessly be led towards socialism. In all this theory the keynote was gradualness; there would be no need ever to do anything to bring the NEP abruptly to an end; it would at last just wither away, as in Marxist doctrine the state itself was ultimately destined to do.

There were, however, two difficulties adverse to the fulfilment of this prospect. The first was the resentment it caused among many Communists, who could not regard it as anything but the result of a humiliating defeat which should be repaired as soon as possible. For members of the Party who had acquired a firm conviction that man's earthly salvation lay only in socialism any survival of capitalism under a nominal dictatorship of the proletariat was an outrage, and the idea of such a state of affairs continuing for an indefinite period in the future was intolerable. The great personal prestige of Lenin had reconciled them to the necessity of the NEP as a temporary expedient, but only on the understanding that it would be temporary. It must be remembered also that, although the peasants were a majority of the population of Russia, and the Soviet state was supposed to represent the peasants as well as the workers – as symbolized by the emblem of the hammer and sickle – the membership of the Communist Party was almost exclusively of urban middle-class or working-class origin. Kalinin was the only important Bolshevik of peasant origin, and he was regarded almost as if he were some rare wild animal who could be put on show to prove that the Party was entitled to speak for the peasants. The usual Communist attitude towards the peasantry was fundamentally one of dislike and contempt, in line with Marx's impatience with 'rural idiocy'. The Russian Marxists prided themselves on having got rid of the Narodniks' sentimental illusions about the peasant and his natural inclination towards socialism; they knew that what the normal peasant desired was not socialism, but another acre of land for himself. This knowledge did not serve to promote a sympathetic understanding of the peasant and his problems, but caused him to be regarded as a class enemy. The only solution therefore was to deprive him of his property, as the landlords and big capitalists had already been deprived of theirs.

The other great obstacle to the successful operation of the NEP was the economic trend which came to be known as the 'scissors'. The basis of the NEP was the hope that both agriculture and industry would be revived by the working of supply and demand in a free market. But the system could only function if the economic revival was more or less in proportion on both sides of the exchange, and this condition was not fulfilled. Agriculture revived quickly as soon as state requisitioning was abolished and the peasant was allowed to sell his produce in an open market; he could raise production simply by doing more work and taking more trouble over his farming. But industry needed capital in order to revive and not enough capital was forthcoming. The state-owned sector of industry was costly and inefficient, while the private sector created by the NEP did not come up to expectations because the urban 'nepmen', the new class of small business entrepreneurs now tolerated by the proletarian rulers of the state, felt that they had no security for the future and were unwilling to invest such funds as they had in any enterprise which did not yield a quick return. Thus industry failed to keep pace with agriculture, and the prices of farm produce fell on account of its abundance, while scarcity caused those of industrial goods to rise; soon the peasants were responding to the situation by withholding food-stuffs from the market or cutting down production, and by the end of 1927 the amount of food coming into the towns was again declining. The peasants – or at least the more well-to-do peasants classified as *kulaks* – were accused in the Communist Press of 'holding the cities to ransom'. But if there was to be a market economy, it was useless to expect the peasants to feed the towns out of sheer altruism. A solution on the basis of the NEP would have been to give a high priority to the production of goods required by the peasants and thus increase their incentives to production for sale. But there was an alternative with a greater attraction for many Communists: to compel the peasants to enter collective farms where their work would be under state control and it would no longer be possible for them either to cut down production or withhold their product. This policy would have the advantage that in addition to bringing the peasant sector of the economy under control it would enable the state to extract surplus value from the peasantry for the purpose of financing industry, which could then be developed at high speed instead of limping along as it was under the NEP.

That, in spite of all the factors favouring a drive against peasant property, the NEP was maintained intact for seven years after its adoption in 1921 was due mainly to the relation of political forces centred on personalities within the Communist Party. Lenin during his final illness was worried about the leadership of the Party after his death and he expressed his views on the qualifications of his principal associates in a memorandum for the guidance of the Central Committee or of the next Party Congress whenever that would meet. He dealt with six persons whom he regarded as the most eminent in the Party after himself; they were Trotsky, Stalin, Zinoviev, Kamenev, Bukharin and Pyatakov. He expressed alarm at the strong personal antagonism which had developed between Trotsky and Stalin, and characterized them as follows: [1]

Having become General Secretary, Comrade Stalin has concentrated boundless power in his hands and I am not certain he can always use this power with sufficient caution.... [Trotsky] is, I think, the most able person in the present Central Committee, but he also has an exceptionally extensive self-confidence and an exceptional attraction to the purely administrative side of affairs. These qualities of the two most prominent leaders of the present Central Committee might inadvertently lead to a split, and if our party does not take measures to prevent this, the split might arise unexpectedly.

In this memorandum, which was written on 24 December 1923, Lenin appears to be trying to hold the balance as evenly as he can between Stalin and Trotsky, but on 4 January 1924, just over a fortnight before he died, he added a postscript recommending that Stalin be removed from the post of General Secretary of the Party on the ground that he was 'too rude' to be suitable for that position. Stalin's growing power was in fact based on this office, which had not originally been regarded as in any way conferring a leadership of the Party, but simply as an instrument of the organization of the Party under the conditions of its existence since the capture of the Russian state. What none of the Party leaders, with the exception of Stalin, seems to have realized is that the capture of state power had fundamentally altered the nature of the Party as a political body. Instead of being a small group of dedicated revolutionaries working 'underground' or living in exile abroad it had become an authority in control of the government (and already of a large sector of the economic life) of one of the most populous nations of the world, and this function was regarded as being a permanent one since no other party could be allowed to take it away from the 'vanguard of

1. Louis Fischer, *The Life of Lenin*, p. 640.

the proletariat'. The Party took upon itself the task not only of laying down the policies to be pursued by the ministers of the state government (whom it appointed) but also of supervising directly through its members all branches of civil, military and economic administration, while at the same time carrying on a continual agitation among the masses of the people in order to impel them towards the socialist objective. Such a vast enterprise required not only a Party much larger in numbers than that of 1917, but a far more complex organization than had been needed by a group of men with nothing to do except to distribute an illegal newspaper and surreptitiously make converts to the faith. It had indeed now to have its own bureaucracy of full-time professional organizers and propagandists forming a hierarchy of centrally controlled secretaries in thousands of branches and sub-branches of the Party extending over the whole area of the Soviet Union from the Gulf of Finland to Kamchatka. This was the 'apparatus' and the man who directed it could use it to gain power over the Party itself, for through the branch secretaries, who were nominated by him and dependent on him for their careers, he could influence decisively the elections to Party Congresses and thus indirectly also the composition of the Central Committee to be elected by a Party Congress. The 'Old Bolsheviks', the men who had been in the leading ranks of the Party in 1917, did not realize until it was too late the power which Stalin was obtaining from his position as General Secretary. Had the Party followed Lenin's advice and removed him from the post in 1924, when his power was not yet fully grown, the future fantastic development of his personal despotism might have been avoided. But Stalin was resolved to thwart any move to deprive him of the office and he was extremely skilful in tactical political combinations. In order to attack Trotsky, who initially had great prestige in the Party and was the most obvious heir to the mantle of Lenin, Stalin allied himself with Zinoviev and Kamenev, who were both jealous of Trotsky, and formed with them a clique known as the Troika,[2] which was strong enough to dominate Party affairs. Both Zinoviev and Kamenev had bases of power in the Party which were to some extent comparable to Stalin's for they headed the Party organizations of Leningrad (as Petrograd was renamed after Lenin's death) and Moscow respectively, and these domains resisted penetration by Stalin's apparatus. Ideologically the Troika's campaign against Trotsky was determined by a reaction to his special views; he urged a higher tempo of industrialization and restrictions on the economic activities of the peasants, so the Troika stood firm on the NEP, which was invested with the sacred authority of the dead Lenin. Trotsky was intellectually far superior to either Stalin or Zinoviev, but he showed very little skill in the complicated in-fighting which followed. In 1925 Zinoviev and Kamenev broke with Stalin, not so much on account of any differences on policy as because Stalin was trying to obtain control of their private organizational domains in Leningrad and Moscow; once the Troika had been dissolved, they joined forces politically with Trotsky, but the co-operation was never very close. From 1925 to 1927 Stalin continued the contest against both the Trotsky and Zinoviev factions with the support of the stalwarts of the NEP – Bukharin, whom Lenin described as 'the most valuable and the most distinguished theoretician of the Party', and Rykov, who had been appointed Lenin's successor as Chairman of the Council of People's Commissars.

The fight was over by the end of 1927. Stalin with the aid of his apparatus packed two Party Congresses and the Central Committees elected by them and crushed the Left Opposition as a factional grouping formed in violation of Party discipline. Trotsky was first banished to Alma Ata in Central Asia and was then allowed to go

2. A *troika* was a team of three horses drawing an old-fashioned Russian sleigh.

into exile abroad in 1929; he never returned to Russia, though he survived until he was assassinated by one of Stalin's agents in 1940. Zinoviev and Kamenev were expelled from the Party but were readmitted after humiliating capitulations as Party members without any positions of power; they were finally put to death by Stalin in 1936.

Having thus defeated his most formidable political rivals, Stalin was free in 1928 to determine Party policy as he wished in relation to the NEP and peasant property; he turned sharply to the left, discarding the NEP and launching a grandiose project for high-speed industrialization, to be accompanied by forcible collectivization of peasant agriculture. It has often been regarded as a puzzle why Stalin from being a defender of the NEP suddenly swung to the extreme opposite and initiated what became virtually a civil war against the peasantry. To explain his action it is necessary to take account of the predisposition to violence that was inherent in his character. He was determined to conquer where Lenin had failed, to break the recalcitrance of the peasants and end by a ruthless use of force the compromise which had been the essence of the NEP. Further he saw that a new militant phase of the revolution afforded the best opportunity to rally the Party under his own leadership. In the words of Professor L. Schapiro: [3]

All Communists were agreed in principle in 1928 on the urgent need to develop industry. But there was disagreement on the question of tempo – how fast it was possible to do it? – and its corollary – the extent to which it was permissible to do it at the expense of the peasants.... If he is to be condemned for his inhumanity, he must at all events be given credit for his courage. Yet the very enormity of the task on which he now embarked in some ways insured him against opposition from within.... In conditions of comparative peace and harmony, Stalin's unpopular organizational talents might well

3. L. Schapiro, *The Communist Party of the Soviet Union*, pp. 378 and 383.

seem no longer so essential to the Party for its own survival in power, and other leaders might then come to the fore.

It was to be a revolution from above, backed by the full power of the state. Communist emissaries were sent from the cities into the countryside to talk the peasants into the 'voluntary' surrender of their property to the collective farms, but if they met with resistance they could invoke the aid of special detachments of the internal security troops of the G P U equipped with tanks, artillery and machine-guns. Those classified as *kulaks* were in any case to be driven out of the villages; they were not even to be allowed to join the collective farms, but were to be moved into the cities or to sites of new construction projects to provide the additional labour which the planned expansion of industry would require. The so-called middle peasants were to be herded into the collective farms, but where they offered resistance they too would be deported to forced labour. It was estimated that with the intended mechanization agriculture could be carried on with far fewer hands than had hitherto been engaged on it, while a much larger force would be needed in industry, so that a big transfer of population from the countryside was in any case desirable and this could be combined with measures for crushing the peasant resistance to collectivization. Once the peasants were in the collectives, they could be made not only to provide the towns with adequate supplies of food at low prices to be fixed by the state, but also to contribute surpluses of grain, butter and sugar which could be exported, together with petrol and timber, to pay for the massive imports of capital goods from abroad needed for the rapid industrialization of the country.

In the years from 1929 to 1933 this immense design was carried out as far as Stalin's will, supported by the fanatical enthusiasm of militant Communists and the ruthless brutality of the security police, could put it into effect. It achieved spectacular successes of industrialization; new power stations, steel plants and engineering works sprang up out of nowhere with a phenomenal speed of growth and Russia's output of coal, iron ore, oil and non-ferrous metals was rapidly increased. The original figures for the First Five-year Plan as worked out by relatively cautious economists in 1929 were soon discarded in favour of more ambitious targets which were then repeatedly raised; the slogan of the day was that 'there are no fortresses which Bolsheviks cannot take'. According to a historian of the period: [4]

Before the year 1930 ended, an order was issued to extend the plans and speed up their application. The fixing of new objectives to be attained in production and in construction work became an all-absorbing everyday task, a kind of collective mania.... The First Five-year Plan was no longer mentioned. No doubts were allowed as to it being accomplished, and even surpassed, in four years. Everyone was plunged into calculations concerning the Second Five-year Plan, to cover the period from January 1933 to the end of 1937. During that period all the capitalist countries, including America, would certainly be left far behind. The future was read in figures, as playing cards are used for fortune-telling, and the figures docilely obeyed the desire of man.

But the peasant called a halt to these soaring flights of the urban imagination. His active resistance to collectivization was indeed crushed; thousands of recalcitrants were killed and hundreds of thousands were deported to forced labour camps or dumped on the outskirts of the new industrial cities such as Magnitogorsk to live in tents and shacks – there was no housing for them – and provide the cheapest of cheap labour for building projects. But if the peasant could not oppose the government in arms he could practise a passive resistance and he did. Vast numbers of horses, cattle, sheep and pigs were killed and eaten so that they were no longer there to be handed over to the collectives, and

4. N. de Basily, *Russia under Soviet Rule*, p. 263.

many of those which were handed over soon died of neglect as the peasants took no further interest in them. The decrease of livestock was prodigious; the number of horses fell from 34 million in 1929 to 16 million in 1933 and that of cattle from 68 million in 1929 to 38 million in 1933. The livestock decline involved not only supplies of meat, milk, butter, wool and leather, but even traction on the farms; the supply of tractors which were to mechanize farming had fallen short of the plan and many of those which were delivered were soon ruined by inexpert use, so that in some areas there were no longer any horses, but not yet any tractors, and the ploughs had to be pulled by the peasants themselves. The general mood of the peasants was one of sullen apathy and its effect on agriculture was compounded by the incompetence of most of the collective farm managements, for nearly all the most successful farmers had been eliminated as *kulaks* and the collectives were being run for the most part by men whose only qualification was skill in jumping on the political bandwagon. By the end of 1932 famine had returned to Russia – or more particularly to the Ukraine; during the winter and in the spring of 1933 great numbers of peasants starved to death. It was the peasants who died and not the workers in the towns, for the state continued to take out of the countryside enough to meet a basic food ration in the towns – and also something for export. A decree was issued prescribing the death penalty for the 'stealing' of grain by the peasants who produced it, and it was vigorously enforced. But mere ferocity of legislation could not revive agriculture. By 1933 it had to be recognized that the economy had undergone an utterly unbalanced development. A great heavy industry had been created, but at the cost of a decline in agriculture, acute shortages of consumer goods and a general impoverishment of the population. The industrial workers as well as the peasants were worse off in terms of real incomes in 1933 than they had been in 1929. The only social group that was definitely better off was that of high Party and state officials; to retain their loyalty and stimulate their zeal for development of the economy Stalin had rewarded them with greatly increased incomes made up of high salaries, perquisites and bonuses. The Communist Party was emerging as a new ruling class with economic advantages for its members corresponding to their monopoly of political power. But all was not well even for the new 'boyars of the bureaucracy'. In Soviet society as it had now been transformed by Stalin's revolution from above the tensions were not less but greater than they had been in the era of the NEP, and the system of violence and terror which Stalin had used for four years to coerce the masses of the Russian people was soon to be turned by him inward against the Party itself.

10.   Stalin and the Great Purge

In January 1934 the Seventeenth Congress of the C P S U
(the Communist Party of the Soviet Union) was held in
Moscow. It called itself the Congress of Victors because
the great programme of collectivizing agriculture and
expanding industry under the First Five-year Plan was
supposed to have been triumphantly achieved. There was
apparently a complete unanimity of members of the
Congress in support of Stalin and his policies. Several
former leaders of groups within the Party which had been
at one time or another opposed to Stalin – Zinoviev,
Kamenev, Bukharin, Pyatakov, Rykov and Radek – made
penitent speeches in which they admitted that Stalin
had always been right and they had been wrong. But
behind the appearance of what had come to be styled
the 'monolithic unity' of the Party there was still conflict,
and a conflict perhaps more dangerous to Stalin's supremacy than the overt opposition with which he had
previously had to contend, because resistance to his arbitrary personal rule was now coming from within the
bloc of those who had hitherto been his supporters.
Schapiro thus explains how this new situation had
arisen: [1]

As the years wore on (from 1929) to an ever-mounting cres-
cendo of self-congratulation from the Party leaders, exaggera-
ted claims of success, faked statistics and exhortation to yet
greater efforts, the more sober realities of the situation produced a corresponding depression. In place of the promised
plenty, there was food shortage, accompanied by strict rationing, especially marked during the famine year of 1932–3. The
rapid influx of the peasants into the towns, which were unpre-

1. L. Schapiro, *The Communist Party of the Soviet Union*, p. 387.

pared to receive them, contributed to the lowering of the standard of living which had made so substantial an advance by the end of the NEP. Absenteeism among workers was soon followed by repressive measures, by direction of labour and strict factory discipline.... By 1931 or 1932, whatever might be said in theory, the relationship between workers and management was undergoing a change which was uncomfortably reminiscent of the picture of exploitation associated with capitalism – even if no one dared say so. All this might have caused little stir had the Plan been successful in achieving its aims. But the results fell far short of the aims that had been set. By 1933 no Communist could have been blamed for doubting whether Stalin and his supporters were really the best men to lead the Party.

It was, indeed, precisely among Stalin's supporters that this doubt was growing in a manner most threatening to his leadership, because these men, after the fall of his former opponents, were now in key positions in the Party. The disaffected Stalinists included Kirov (who now headed the Party organization in Leningrad – the position previously held by Zinoviev), Kossior (who led the Party in the Ukraine), Radzutak, Chubar, Postyshev and others, who, in so far as they could combine politically, were a force to be reckoned with, especially if in a crisis they were to join hands with the former opposition leaders who no longer had positions of authority in the Party but still retained a certain prestige as having been close comrades of Lenin. The Central Committee and Politburo which came out of the Seventeenth Congress contained large elements which were from Stalin's point of view unreliable. Further, the Congress deprived him of his unique authority as General Secretary by appointing four co-equal Secretaries for Party administration – they were to be Stalin, Kirov, Kaganovitch and Zhdanov. Stalin would still have the political advantage in this group, for Kaganovitch and Zhdanov could be reckoned his firm supporters, but he could no longer act simply at his own discretion as unique head of the Secretariat, and there can be no doubt that the Congress intended by this new arrangement to set a limit to his power. The popularity of Kirov with the delegates to the Congress was demonstrated by the ovation he received – a disclosure which could not have failed to arouse alarm in Stalin's jealous and suspicious mind. It is probable in view of what subsequently happened that Stalin fully recognized the danger to his leadership from the new political development and was already planning to deal with it in his own time and in his own way. How he dealt with it was later to be revealed by Khrushchev, who survived the Great Purge because he had always been a devoted Stalinist subservient to his master's will. In the famous secret speech which he delivered to a closed session of the Twentieth Congress of the CPSU in 1956 Khrushchev stated:

... of the 139 members and candidates of the Party's Central Committee who were elected at the Seventeenth Congress 98 persons, i.e. seventy per cent, were arrested and shot.... The same fate met not only the Central Committee members but also the majority of the delegates to the Seventeenth Party Congress. Of 1,966 delegates with either voting or advisory rights 1,108 persons were arrested on charges of counter-revolutionary crimes, i.e. decidedly more than half.

Stalin's solution had at least the merit of a certain simplicity of conception. If a majority of the members of a Party Congress and of the Central Committee which it elected – bodies which theoretically had supreme authority in the Party – were either opposed to Stalin or wavering in their loyalty to him, the difficulty could be overcome by simply putting them to death – a procedure which would not merely eliminate the culprits themselves but would also induce a more suitable frame of mind in those who might subsequently be raised up to fill the places of the dead. This solution came naturally to Stalin because of his innately cruel and vindictive temperament, and he had ready to hand as an instrument a terrorist police force which had been brutalized by five years of punitive expeditions and executions in a wholesale coercion of the masses of the Russian people. He may also have been stimulated in making up his mind to resort to a massacre of his Party comrades by the example of Hitler's successful purge of his insubordinate Nazi followers in the action of 30 June 1934; Krivitsky, the Soviet intelligence agent who defected in 1938, has recorded that Stalin, far from being shocked by Hitler's action, was much impressed by it, and saw in it proof that Hitler really had what it took to govern Germany.

The Great Purge, as it came to be known, nevertheless took the Party by surprise because its members, at least the veterans who had been in it already in 1917, had assumed that, however bitter might be the in-fighting between cliques and factions, they were personally immune from the penalties of imprisonment or death which had been meted out to non-Communist adversaries. Lenin had exhorted his associates to make it a rule that they should never put each other to death because of their quarrels. As a revolutionary with a knowledge of history he remembered the fatal conflicts of the French Revolution when Robespierre had first eliminated his rivals by the guillotine and had then been himself killed by the Thermidorians. Lenin hoped that by imposing a strict discipline on the Party and by providing a disciplinary organ which could act as a court for any charges brought against Party members he could ensure that quarrels would be kept within bounds and essential unity maintained. This organ was the Control Commission, which was independent of the executive authorities of the Party; the secret police, at whose mercy were all inhabitants of the Soviet Union outside the Party, could not arrest a Party member until his case had been heard by the Control Commission or one of its local branches. The members of the Party were thus privileged in that they alone were protected by law against arbitrary repressions by the executive power of the state, though the law which protected them was not the 'law of the land', but consisted of the rules and regulations of the Party itself. As long as the immunity of Party members was maintained in practice, the Soviet political system was an oligarchy, since the monopoly of political life by the Communists as the *parti unique* in effect deprived all citizens outside the Party of all political rights, but the Party itself was governed internally by elected committees which selected delegates to the periodically held Party Congresses.

There were, however, inherent in the system strong factors tending to transform the oligarchy into a personal dictatorship. The rule of the Party, as a small minority of the population seeking to control the lives of all citizens in a manner going far beyond the normal functions of government, required a strong personal leadership to keep the Party together, and this need was greatly increased when its policies involved large-scale coercion and the acute aggravation of social tensions, as in the years from 1929 to 1934. Moreover, while the need for a strong personal leadership increased, so also did the opportunities for building up a position of preponderant personal power within the Party. As has been already pointed out, the nature of the Party had been changed by its capture of the state power, and this was not merely because so many of its members were henceforth performing administrative functions either in the state bureaucracy or in the management of nationalized industry and trade. The whole spirit of the Party underwent a subtle transformation.

Before 1917 it could be said that nobody joined the Party for what he could get out of it in terms of material gain. It was an illegal – or after 1905 semi-legal – organization with no prospect of a capture of political power in the near future, but plenty of risk of imprisonment or exile. It is therefore reasonable to assume that those who joined it were inspired by a genuine political conviction. Some of them, no doubt, were social misfits who would have been frustrated and discontented in whatever kind of society they had been brought up and whose talents were primarily subversive and destructive. But the most eminent Bolsheviks were men who could have made successful and lucrative careers for themselves within the social order of Tsarist Russia if they had been willing to conform to it; there can be no doubt that Lenin, who was trained as a lawyer, would have made his mark in the law courts of St Petersburg, and that Trotsky, with his great literary talent, would have flourished as a writer or a professor of history. If such men renounced the careers which obviously awaited them in order to become penurious 'professional revolutionaries' it was because of political beliefs and the passionate commitment which they inspired. As a consequence of this such men were willing to submit to a quasi-military discipline in order to forward the cause which they had at heart, but only in so far as they could be persuaded that such a discipline was necessary for the end in view. They could not be prevented from speaking their minds if they considered that the Party's policy was wrong, and in the last resort they could leave the Party; there was nothing to stop them.

It was a very different world in which members of the CPSU moved a decade and a half after the conquest of power; whether the veterans of the Party liked it or not, it had become a world of 'jobs for the boys'. And all jobs of every kind. Not only posts in the Party apparatus, now paid at rates which would have supported half a dozen professional revolutionaries in the old days, but all posts in the state administration, in the police and the army, in every branch of the economy from the management of steel plants and oilfields to the directing of collective farms, and in all the professions – writers and journalists, scientists and teachers, lawyers and doctors, artists and actors – all now depended on the omnipotent party-state for employment and promotion. The Communists had originally laid down the principle – derived from the ideology of the Paris Commune of 1871 – that a Party member holding a state office should not be paid more than the wages of a skilled worker. A few civil servants, industrial managers, engineers and others taken over from the old bourgeois society and employed by the new regime because of their special expertise were paid more because it was recognized that persons of bourgeois mentality had to have such monetary incentives, but just for this reason they were despised by the exponents of the new socialist morality and were contrasted with men of revolutionary conviction who were indifferent to personal comfort and were devoted to a selfless service of society. Soon, however, Party members grew accustomed to the idea that they were entitled to certain privileges not available to the rest of the population as regards food (in periods of rationing), housing and holidays; these privileges were at first defended on the ground that Party members must be kept in full health for the many exacting tasks imposed on them, but before long they were taken for granted and their scope tended to increase. Finally in 1932 even the conventional form of simple living for Party members was swept away; the higher officialdom now received incomes five, ten or twenty times those of the most prosperous factory workers and Party members were encouraged to aim at such posts. The old idea that they ought not to be better off than the proletariat of which they were the 'vanguard' was now denounced as 'petty-bourgeois egalitarianism'.

There were many even among the 'Old Bolsheviks' – those who had been already members of the Party in 1917 – who were not averse to this trend and who came to the conclusion in their middle age that they deserved a comfortable life as a reward for the hardships and anxieties they had suffered in their youth for the sake of the cause. But if this disposition to profit personally from the revolution was fairly widespread among the

Old Bolsheviks, it was almost universal among those who joined the Party after it was already in power – or at any rate after 1920, when the Whites had been defeated and there was no longer the risk of being executed by the counter-revolution. The Party had now become the road to material advancement and social status – and the only road – for every young man or woman with an ambition to get on in the world, or merely to emerge from the poverty which was the lot of the vast majority of the Russian people. The Party could select its new recruits, it imposed courses of indoctrination and tests of work before admission, and the novice was under continual surveillance by his comrades and the local Party secretary, liable to expulsion at any moment for some breach of discipline or failure to give satisfaction. But no sort of test could ensure that the candidate was disinterestedly convinced of the truth of Communist doctrine and was not entering the Party in order to embark on a profitable official career. Such a career depended on attracting the favourable notice of superiors who could recommend for promotion, in other words on finding a patron. Thus arose the system of *chevstvo* or patronage in the Party, whereby leading Party members holding key posts either in the apparatus or in the state administration worked for the advancement of those whom they favoured and expected in return their support in factional conflicts.

More and more, therefore, these conflicts came to be not merely differences of opinion, even as accentuated by personal likes and dislikes; they became rivalries of material interest with the spoils of office as the prize of victory. In the struggle for power the General Secretary had the biggest patronage and this, as we have seen, was the basis of Stalin's predominance, yet it did not by itself ensure a complete and permanent supremacy, and when the Seventeenth Congress put the office in commission among four individuals it restricted his patronage. Moreover, as long as the Party membership as a whole accepted Lenin's rule that a Communist should never be put to death for a merely political opposition to the current Party leadership, it was impossible for Stalin to go beyond the influence he could exert by reason of his patronage and eliminate finally those who opposed him. Fortunately for Stalin, however, an opportunity presented itself within a year of the Seventeenth Congress to accuse his enemies of having been the first to violate Lenin's commandment.[2] Among the members of the Party in Leningrad – where the Party organization headed by Kirov was virtually independent of Stalin's apparatus – there was a young man called Nikolayev who had become acutely discontented with the way things were going both in the Party and in the country generally. Since he talked openly about his grievances and confided to his friends his opinion that assassinations such as had been carried out in the nineteenth century by the Narodnik terrorists were now again needed to deliver Russia from a new oppression, it was not surprising that he attracted the notice of the secret police and that one of his friends was persuaded to act as an *agent provocateur*. This friend gave him a revolver and he entered the office of the Party headquarters in Leningrad with the intention of shooting Kirov; a policeman on duty arrested him, but he was released on orders from above, and a month later, on 1 December 1934, he tried again and was this time successful. Stalin's most formidable rival was thus removed, but not by any action which could be traced to Stalin himself; he professed the greatest grief and indignation and hurried to Leningrad to conduct in person an investigation of the crime. His intention appears to have been to induce Nikolayev

2. The murder of Kirov remains a historical mystery because, as Khrushchev pointed out in his anti-Stalin speech at the Twentieth Congress, everyone who was even remotely qualified as a witness had perished in the Great Purge. It is probable, however, that the main facts were as related by A. Orlov in his book *The Secret History of Stalin's Crimes*.

to admit that he had planned the assassination at the instigation of Zinoviev, but Nikolayev was completely recalcitrant and showed that he was fully aware that the revolver had been given him on the instructions of the secret police. Since he could not be expected to refrain from saying so if he were given a public trial, he was tried *in camera* and executed along with thirteen other persons who had formerly belonged to Zinoviev's faction and were alleged to be accomplices. Zinoviev and Kamenev were arrested, but all they could be persuaded initially to admit was that they had 'ideologically' influenced the assassin by their criticism of Stalin. They were sentenced respectively to ten and five years' imprisonment. But this was only a beginning. What Stalin needed was first that they should confess to having directly organized the murder of Kirov, thus making themselves liable to the death penalty, and second, that they should implicate other prominent opponents of Stalin as having been involved in the plot so that they also could be put to death. For this purpose time was needed and expert interrogators of the GPU – which in 1934 had been transformed into the People's Commissariat of Internal Affairs, the NKVD – worked on Zinoviev, Kamenev and a number of other arrested Communists in prison for eighteen months without cessation, using the special methods for breaking the wills of prisoners which had been tried out in a series of 'confession trials' since 1928. By August 1936 Zinoviev and the others had confessed to having organized the murder of Kirov on the instructions of the exiled Trotsky (then in Norway) and they repeated their confessions in open court; they were all sentenced to death and shot. In their testimony they also implicated Bukharin, Rykov and members of the Right faction, who had continued to advocate the NEP line after Stalin had turned away from it. These were duly arrested, but were released after the Central Committee had voted by a two-thirds majority against committing them for 'trial'. It was a setback for Stalin, but only a temporary one. If a majority of the Central Committee were against killing Bukharin and Rykov, then they must be killed too. Stalin withdrew to Sochi on the coast of the Black Sea and from there sent a telegram to the Politburo on 23 September demanding that his henchman Yezhov should be appointed People's Commissar of Internal Affairs in place of Yagoda, who, he said, 'has definitely shown himself to be incapable of unmasking the Trotskyite–Zinovievite *bloc*'. The Politburo, in which Stalin's supporters were a bare majority, gave their assent to the new appointment and it was decisive. Yagoda had for many years trimmed politically between the factions of the Party, never committing himself finally to any; Yezhov was a creature of Stalin's personal secretariat, owing his career entirely to Stalin and ready to do whatever his master ordered.

Now all the barriers were down and the great massacre began. Arrests were made at all levels of the Party from the Central Committee down to the newest recruits in the local branches. Any record of association with opposition groups, of adverse voting in elections or of remarks critical of Stalin and his policies was enough to warrant arrest, to be followed either by execution or by a long sentence in a concentration camp. The most prominent of those arrested were subjected to special treatment to prepare them for making confessions in open court; persons of less political importance were tortured to compel them to sign confessions for the record, but were not produced in open court; the unimportant ones never received any kind of trial, but were merely informed what their sentences were. The total number of those arrested remains unknown, but it was probably somewhere between a quarter and a half of the total membership of the Party.

The Red Army provided a special problem, for there was a danger that mass arrests of officers might provoke armed resistance and a military *coup d'état*. Moreover, Marshal Voroshilov, who was People's Commissar for War, was unreliable from Stalin's point of view, for, although he was a political supporter of Stalin, he had too much solidarity with the professional officers to be likely to consent to a purge unless there appeared to be an adequate reason for it. But Stalin was determined to purge the Army as well as the Party, for he knew that he had been bitterly criticized in high military circles; the merciless repressions of the peasantry had affected the morale of conscripts to the Army from the villages, and the Army in 1932 had had to give up its stocks of grain, held for a war emergency, in order to relieve the famine which Stalin's ruthlessness had brought about. Moreover, the Red Army's most popular and able leader, Marshal Tukhachevsky, had a personal feud with Stalin going back to the period of the civil war. In order to have a pretext for dealing with Tukhachevsky and other generals whom the reports of his spies indicated as malcontent, Stalin resorted to an extremely ingenious device.[3] In Paris there lived an exiled White Russian general of the name of Skoblin who was in the pay of the Soviet N K V D and was also a secret agent of the Nazi German S D. Through Yezhov, Skoblin was instructed to feed false information alleging that Tukhachevsky was a German agent to the Czech intelligence service. This he did and President Beneš innocently passed on the information to Moscow. Skoblin, however, did even better than this; he suggested to the S D that evidence should also be forthcoming directly from Germany. Heydrich obtained the approval of Hitler for the project – which was seen as likely to result in a weakening of the military power of the Soviet Union – and a correspondence was forged by the S D to show that Tukhachevsky had sold

3. The facts with regard to the Tukhachevsky affair only became known after the Second World War when they were revealed by Hoettl, Schellenberg and Behrens who were involved in the operation on the German side. Three White Russians who planted false information on behalf of General Skoblin also testified. Skoblin, wanted by the French police in connexion with the kidnapping of General Miller in September 1937, fled to Spain, was taken on a Russian ship and was never seen again.

to Germany the mobilization plans of the Red Army. When the forged documents were ready, they were purchased for three million roubles by the NKVD and presented by Stalin to Voroshilov and the Politburo as irrefutable proofs of guilt.

Tukhachevsky and several other generals were arrested and shot. Eight generals were persuaded to act as a court-martial and six of these were afterwards arrested and shot as well. The purge was extended through all officer ranks of the Red Army. Fifty-seven out of eighty-five corps commanders and 110 out of 195 divisional commanders were reported to have been executed. When in 1941 Hitler attacked the Soviet Union the Red Army had still not yet recovered from the ferocious bloodletting.

What Stalin wanted was a Party and an Army completely subservient to his will and purged of all critical or independent thought. The wholesale killing which went on until the end of 1938 removed everyone who had any oppositional record and profoundly intimidated those who remained. Early in 1939 Stalin considered it safe to hold elections for a new Party Congress, the Eighteenth. Every delegate who attended this Congress bore in mind the fact that more than half the delegates to the last Congress had been shot. When their beloved leader appeared on the platform all the delegates rose to their feet and cheered. The cheering went on and on, for no one wished to be noticed as being the first to stop. Stalin had no rival now; he was an absolute monarch and his revolutionary comrades – or rather those of them who had survived – had become his courtiers.

11. The Rise of Communism in China

During the first six years after the Bolshevik capture of power in Russia in 1917 the hopes of the Communists for similar revolutions outside Russia were set primarily on Western Europe. This was in accordance with what had been previously the Marxist theory of revolution – the idea that a socialist revolution would be made by the industrial proletariat which had been created by capitalism and that the more industrialized a country became the nearer it was to revolution. In order to explain the fact that the revolution had come first in Russia, which was industrially not the most developed, but the most backward of the Great Powers of Europe, the theory was modified to provide for a first outbreak of the revolution in a country which was not the most advanced, if special circumstances had exceptionally weakened the state in that country, but it was still held that this would serve as a 'detonator' for revolutions in the countries which by the orthodox theory were more ripe for the proletarian takeover. The detonator, however, failed to work. The proletariat had taken over the government in Petrograd, but it did not do so in Berlin, Vienna, Paris or London. Soon it became evident that the bourgeois order in Western Europe, even after the disruption and demoralization caused by the First World War, was not going to be quickly or easily overthrown. In North America it was even stronger. The question then arose whether revolutions could be expected in any other part of the world – that is to say, in areas which were economically not more, but less, developed than Russia. The continents of Asia and Africa – except for Japan, which had developed a political and economic system comparable to that of a European country – were everywhere still in a pre-industrial stage; their economies were essentially agrarian, and such elements of modern industry as existed in them in the form of railways, docks, mines and light industry factories were usually owned, not by native, but by European, capitalists. Politically most of these countries were under the rule of European states; those which had retained a formal independence, such as Turkey, Persia and China, were in Marxist terms semi-colonial, because of their economic dependence on Western nations. In particular China was subject to various limitations of sovereignty such as extraterritorial consular jurisdictions, leased territories and 'concessions' under foreign administration and the stationing of foreign troops in certain places for the protection of foreign residents and their property.

In these countries important factors of discontent existed – of poverty-stricken peasants against 'feudal' landowners, of rising indigenous bourgeois elements against foreign capitalists or an oppressive native officialdom, of nationalists, especially among the new Western-educated intelligentsia, against foreign rule or political ascendancy. None of these forces was identical with that with which Marxists were primarily concerned – the discontent of industrial workers against the capitalist owners of industry. But they were forces which, if well co-ordinated and organized, might create serious upheavals in Asia and Africa at the expense not only of indigenous native authorities and ruling classes, but also of the Western powers which, whether or not they had full political control over these countries, had large amounts of capital invested in them. Marxists believed that capitalism in the West had become dependent on its investments in colonial and semi-colonial areas of the world, so that if these investments were lost through revolts of the native peoples, it would be greatly weakened and its final crisis brought nearer. It might thus be possible for the Comintern, unable to pierce the ramparts of capitalism in Western Europe or North America, nevertheless to inflict heavy blows against it by destroying its economic power and political holdings in Asia and Africa or at least compelling it to fight expensive wars in order to defend its positions in those continents.

Any Communist activity in essentially pre-industrial countries would, however, have to reckon with the numerical weakness of the industrial working class in their populations. A Communist party in such an environment could only be effective by allying itself with purposes quite different from its own – discontented peasants who wanted to divide up landlords' estates as their own private property and bourgeois nationalists who wanted to get rid of foreign rule or foreign invested capital so as to provide scope for the expansion of a native capitalism. These were allies with whom a unity of common effort might be maintained against the old native ruling classes or against alien colonial rulers, but with whom conflict was inevitable as soon as victory in that struggle was won. The course of events in China was to illustrate in a most striking manner the problem involved in the task of 'making a proletarian revolution without a proletariat'.

The first beginning of Communism in Asia – apart from the territories of the Russian empire in Siberia and Central Asia which were involved in the general course of events in Russia and became parts of the new Soviet Union – was in the Netherlands East Indies, later to become the new national state of Indonesia. The Indonesian Communist Party was founded in 1920 from Europe by the Dutchman Sneevliet, who used the revolutionary pseudonym of Maring. Maring also later played an important part in the founding of the Chinese Communist Party. The way for the latter had been prepared by an agitation among the Chinese intelligentsia which drew its force from the disastrous conditions of Chinese life in the second decade of the twentieth century but had until a very late stage little or nothing to do with

Marxism. In 1912 the Chinese imperial monarchy had been overthrown and replaced by what was theoretically a democratic republic, but no sort of democracy had emerged nor had even the unity of the Chinese state been preserved; the country became a prey to the factions formed by military governors of provinces who became virtually independent and recruited badly disciplined troops as their private armies. The condition of the peasant masses grew worse; they were in many areas overcrowded on the land available, bore a crushing burden of taxes and rents, and had lost through the imports of cheap foreign goods the earnings from handicraft cottage industries by which they had formerly supplemented their meagre livelihood from agriculture. The conditions created by the arbitrary rule of the 'war-lords' were adverse to the growth of a native capitalist industry, so that Chinese in possession of capital preferred to put it into the foreign-administered settlements or buy land rather than invest it in industrial undertakings. In addition to this chaotic internal situation – and partly because of it – China was beset from without by severe pressures from foreign nations, though these came no longer so much from the European powers which had encroached on China in the nineteenth century as from their faithfully imitative pupil Japan. The latter had taken advantage of the European war of 1914 to press on China the so-called Twenty-one Demands, most of which China had to accept as a result of an ultimatum; subsequently Japan was able to obtain, as a price for her naval assistance against the German submarine campaign, the consent of Britain and France to post-war retention by Japan of the German leased territory of Kiaochow, which her troops had captured in 1914 – a deal to which the United States government finally gave endorsement at the Paris Peace Conference. The national humiliation of having a piece of Chinese territory transferred by deals among foreign powers, added on to the exasperation felt by patriotic educated Chinese at the internal condition of the country, led in 1919 to the protest riots of students in Peking known as the May Fourth Movement. There was as yet no Communist Party, but the news of the Russian Revolution had already made an impact on the more radical section of the Chinese intelligentsia, and the fact that the new Soviet Russia was not represented at the Paris Peace Conference exempted it in Chinese sentiment from the opprobrium which was now attached to all the nations that were signatories of the Treaty of Versailles.

It was in these circumstances that a number of Chinese intellectuals began to be attracted by Marxism, not as one of the many forms of social and political theory imported from the West and contributing to the ferment of ideas among the small Western-educated academic and professional class, but as the creed of the new Soviet regime which had won their sympathy and admiration. They began to make a study of Marxism, but they came to it with minds formed in a Chinese environment and preoccupied with problems other than those which stimulated the thoughts of Marx and Engels in Western Europe or even of Plekhanov and Lenin in Russia. Li Ta-chao,[1] who was to be one of the two most prominent leaders in the first phase of the Chinese Communist movement, was inspired by sentiments of national patriotism such as would have been regarded with the greatest mistrust by any European Marxist before 1917; a popular revolution was for him not so much a matter of social progress as a means by which China could sweep away a corrupt and inefficient ruling class and recover her ancient national greatness, on which the more competent powers of the West had so ruthlessly trampled. Moreover, when he contemplated a popular revolution it was the peasants rather than the urban workers that he had in mind. Coming himself from a prosperous peasant stock and having virtually no contacts with the

1. A good biography is provided my Maurice Meisner, *Li Ta-chao and the Origins of Chinese Marxism*, Harvard U.P., 1967.

industrial working class – then confined to Shanghai and a few other places – he saw the creative upheaval as coming from the farms and not the factories of China. He was not destined to live long; he was put to death by soldiers of the Manchurian war-lord Chang Tso-lin in 1927. But his attitude of mind persisted, for his was the most important formative influence on the mind of a library assistant of Peking National University, where Li Ta-chao was librarian concurrently with being a professor of the university. The assistant librarian's name was Mao Tse-tung and he was a peasant's son from Hunan province. Mao had already been prominent in local radical politics before he came to Peking, but it was in Peking that he became a convert to Marxism through the Marxist Research Society which was founded by Li in 1918.

The Chinese Communist Party did not exist as an organized body until July 1921, when its first Congress met secretly in Shanghai, composed of two delegates from each of six small groups which had already been formed in Chinese cities, one delegate from a group of Chinese in Japan, and two representatives of the Comintern, a Russian named Voitinsky and the Maring who had already launched a Communist Party in Java. Mao was one of the thirteen Chinese members of the Congress, but Li Ta-chao himself did not attend. There were only some seventy members in the whole of China, but this did not prevent the Congress from deciding that it represented the proletariat and would have no links with any other party or group. The attitude of the Comintern was somewhat different. The CPSU was glad to have a Communist Party in China, even if it were only of minute size, but in its concern for the security of the Soviet Union against Japan was anxious to arrive at a friendly understanding with any faction in China which could be used as a counterweight to the power of Japan's protégé, the Manchurian war-lord Chang Tso-lin. After attending the founding Congress of the Chinese Communist Party, therefore, Maring visited two war-lords of Central China in whom Moscow was interested and then met Sun Yat-sen at Kweilin in December 1921. Sun, the leader of the bourgeois nationalist party known as the Kuomintang, had played an important part in the overthrow of the monarchy in 1911–12, and after the partition of China among the war-lords had established himself at Canton as head of a 'government', but as he maintained his local power by hiring mercenary troops whom he did not really control, he was regarded originally by the Chinese Communists as no better than a war-lord himself. On Maring's advice, however, Moscow came to the conclusion that the Kuomintang would be the best ally for the Soviet Union in China and it was decided to bring about an alliance between the Kuomintang and the Communists to carry on a joint struggle against the war-lords and also against British and Japanese influence in China. After some reluctance on both sides the alliance was negotiated. Its terms were peculiar; the Communists were to become individually members of the Kuomintang and thus be, so to speak, inside it, while at the same time the Kuomintang was to be reorganized as a party on the advice of organizational experts sent from Moscow and a Party army was to be trained by a military mission sent from the Soviet Union. In this arrangement there can be no doubt that each side hoped to use and in the end to get the better of the other; the Kuomintang hoped by means of it to get Soviet advice and arms and Communist-influenced working-class support in Shanghai and other cities, and the Comintern and the Chinese Communists hoped to penetrate the Kuomintang organization and take it over from within.

For a time the Kuomintang–Communist coalition proved very successful. The Kuomintang had strong support in the Chinese middle class; the Communists gained a substantial working-class following in Canton and Shanghai; both parties joined in a high-powered propaganda campaign, assisted by expert Russian advice,

against both the Chinese war-lords and the foreign imperialists. An incident in Shanghai in 1925, when a strike
in a Japanese-owned factory in the International Settlement led to shooting by a British-officered police unit,
provided the occasion for a furious nation-wide denunciation of the 'unequal treaties' and the conditions which
made it possible for Chinese to be shot down by foreigners
on Chinese territory. The war-lords and their phantom
government in Peking were denounced not so much for
their misdeeds in the internal administration of China
as for their indifference and incompetence in passively
putting up with foreign encroachments on the country's
sovereignty. In the spring of 1926 (Sun Yat-sen having
died the year before), the Kuomintang launched a military
expedition with its new army under the command of
General Chiang Kai-shek. The aim was to advance north
from Canton and bring first Central and then North
China under the control of the Canton government,
which was directed by the coalition of the Kuomintang
and Communist parties. The Canton army was a force
of a type quite different from any of the armies of the
war-lords; it had not only received a good military
training from the Soviet mission but it had also been
imbued by indoctrination with a sense of political purpose entirely lacking in the *condottieri* who served the
war-lords. Moreover, virtually the whole population was
against the war-lords and the demagogic propaganda of
the Kuomintang–Communist coalition evoked a vast
popular enthusiasm, so that everywhere the advancing
army was assisted by the people. Cities were captured one
after another – Changsha, Hankow, Nanking and finally
Shanghai, the wealthiest and most populous city of
China, which the Communist-organized General Labour
Union captured from within even before Chiang's army
overcame the resistance of the troops defending it. But
the coalition did not survive the taking of Shanghai. The
influence obtained by the Communists through their
propaganda had become too great to be regarded with

equanimity by the Kuomintang. The support of the masses which had been sought against the war-lords had now turned into a mass movement fired by hopes of an immediate transformation of society and hardly to be controlled even by the Communists themselves, whose leaders, obedient to the directives of the Comintern, were trying to maintain the alliance with the Kuomintang and avoid setting up a rival authority. The right-wing leaders of the Kuomintang, who had the support of most of the officers of the army, decided to move against the Communists before they became too strong. After entering Shanghai with his troops, Chiang Kai-shek took steps to suppress the General Labour Union, and when he met with resistance carried out a massacre of local Communists and workers' pickets. For a while the Kuomintang was split into Right and Left factions, with the Left, which had transferred the seat of government from Canton to Hankow, still keeping up the alliance with the Communists. But in the end, the Left Kuomintang, horrified at a peasant *jacquerie* in Hunan, which the Communists as a party had half-heartedly endorsed rather than led, also turned against them, and crushed them in Hankow and Changsha. In the autumn the Communists in Canton seized and held the city for two days, but Kuomintang troops recaptured it and killed every Communist they captured; the Communists wore no uniforms, but had provided their followers with red scarves the dye of which stained the neck, so that even when the scarves were thrown away the tell-tale marks remained.

Stalin, fundamentally more interested in the alliance with the Kuomintang against Britain and Japan than in the cause of the Chinese Communists, had clung to the inter-party alliance long after it should have been clear that the Kuomintang would seek to destroy their too successful allies. He had dissuaded the Chinese Communist leaders from taking any action to forestall the measures to suppress them and had poured scorn on Trotsky's proposal that the time had come to set up soviets in China. But when both Right and Left factions of the Kuomintang had turned against the Communists, Stalin went to the opposite extreme and instead of dissuading the Communists from any independent action prompted them to the most recklessly aggressive action. The Canton uprising, which had no real chance of success in view of the military strength of the other side, was instigated by the Comintern representatives on the spot, and led only to the death of virtually all the Communists who were in the city at the time.

What then was left after the suppression of the Chinese Communists in the few cities in which they had a following? What was left was a peasant insurrection in which the Communists had initially taken but little interest, but which was not crushed when the Communists were suppressed in Shanghai, Hankow and Canton. Its leader was Mao Tse-tung, himself of Hunanese peasant origin, who took the unorthodox view that the peasants were no mere auxiliaries in a Communist revolution, but were actually more important than the urban workers for making one. Mao was not yet the leader of the Chinese Party and he could not at that time sustain his views against the orthodox leadership backed by the full authority of the Comintern; he even had to make a recantation under threat of expulsion from the Party. But reality was on his side; after 1927 the insurgent peasants were in the field as an armed revolutionary force whereas the urban workers were not. It was all very well to keep on saying that the workers would make the revolution, but it was only the peasants who were actually doing so. Little by little theory was made to conform to the facts of the situation; the revolution had to be led by the urban working class, but the urban working class was represented by the Communist Party, and if the Communists were leading a peasant rebellion, then the principle of proletarian leadership was still being maintained. This was Marxism with a difference, and the difference was that a revolution inspired by Marx and Lenin was being made in a country which was far less industrialized than Russia had been in 1917 and did not correspond at all to the society imagined in *Das Kapital* as the outcome of the economic development of capitalism.

12.   The Idea of the Popular Front

When on 30 January 1933 Hitler became Chancellor of Germany, the Communists, both in Germany and elsewhere, were faced with a new situation, which, if they did not appreciate it immediately, was forced on their attention in the months that followed. His appointment was disastrous for the Communists in two ways. Within Germany he set to work to destroy the Communist Party, breaking up its organization, seizing its funds and rounding up its more active members for incarceration in 'protective custody'. But his anti-Communist action was not confined to the Germans. He made it plain that he had not forgotten the project he had discussed in *Mein Kampf* for creating a great *Lebensraum* for Germany in Russia and its 'borderlands' (which meant especially the Ukraine). The Nazi victory, therefore, implied not merely the destruction of the largest Communist Party in Europe to the west of the Soviet frontier, but also a threat of war to the Soviet Union itself, as soon as the Nazis should have carried out that rearmament of Germany in defiance of the Treaty of Versailles which was their preliminary objective.

For Communists who still had minds of their own, and had not yet conditioned themselves to accept all Stalin's actions as inspired by an infallible wisdom, he could not but be held to have incurred a grave responsibility for what had happened in Germany. Ever since 1928 the line given to Communist parties in Europe through the Comintern under Stalin's guidance had been one of 'Left extremism', a policy of refusal to enter into political alliances with any non-Communist party and of particular hostility to the leaders of the democratic socialist or 'reformist' parties – the Social Democrats in Germany, the Socialists in France and the Labour Party in Britain. This course was in conformity with Stalin's domestic policy in so far as it was one which presented him as the uncompromising, dedicated revolutionary, the man who would make no concessions to the bourgeoisie or to cowards and waverers. He would make an end of all collaboration with reformists in the politics of other countries just as he had made an end of the NEP inside Russia. But between 1928 and 1933 a great change took place in the situation with which the Comintern had to deal in the country which had always occupied first place in Communist hopes for European revolution – that is to say, in Germany. In 1928 there was indeed no prospect of an early opportunity for revolutionary action; the German economy had revived after the inflation crisis of 1923 and had undergone a new expansion with US financial aid, while politically the democratic Weimar Republic appeared to be firmly established and far too strong to be overthrown by any proletarian insurrection. But then came the great economic depression starting with the US stock market crash in the autumn of 1929 and spreading to Europe in the following year; bank failures, bankruptcies and mass unemployment soon created a vast infection of discontent and despair which threatened the foundations of the social and political order. In these circumstances the Communists increased their following and their voting strength. But the gains of the hitherto insignificant National Socialist Party were far greater and they had what the Communists lacked – contacts within the citadels of existing authority, the bureaucracy, the army and big business. The question thus arose for the Communists whether to maintain their splendid isolation in German politics or to join hands with the democratic parties in order to preserve the Weimar constitution and avert a Nazi dictatorship. Under the political democracy of Weimar the Communists might have no chance of capturing power, but at least they had a legal existence as a party, with the right to carry on open political activity and propaganda. It could be argued that since these liberties were now threatened the Communists should for the time being make a pact with all parties prepared to resist a Nazi takeover of the state. The Nazis, even in alliance with the Nationalists, were a minority in the Reichstag right up to the time when Hitler was made Chancellor, and until the summer of 1932 the Social Democrats controlled the government of Prussia, the largest of the federal constituent states of Weimar Germany. But the Communists continued an implacable opposition to the Social Democrats and to all the parties which were trying to preserve democracy in Germany. This was more than a mere blind persistence in a policy which had been adopted when circumstances were different. Stalin had two reasons which from his point of view were good ones for wishing to see the Weimar Republic destroyed. In the first place it could be anticipated that the collapse of democracy would be irremediably disastrous for the German Social Democrats as a reformist, liberal-minded Menshevik party, but it would not be fatal for the German Communists, because alongside their overt legal activities they had always maintained a conspiratorial secret organization and it would not hurt them too much to go underground for a time. Secondly, Stalin apparently shared the belief entertained by von Papen and the conservatives who formed a coalition with Hitler in 1933 that he would become their prisoner and that ultimate power in a Nazi–Nationalist regime would be wielded by the Reichswehr generals who favoured a Russo–German military alliance. Some inconvenience for the German Communists would be a small price to pay for a firmer relationship with the German army and the elimination of those elements in Germany which desired a reconciliation with France and Britain.

If, as the available evidence indicates, these were the most important considerations in deciding the line of

Communist policy in Germany from 1930, when the Nazis scored their first big electoral successes, to 1933, when Hitler became Chancellor, the sequel was very disappointing. The Social Democrats were indeed effectively suppressed, but so also were the Communists, for the measures taken by the Nazis to pull up the roots of the Party organization were far more thorough and ruthless than had been anticipated. The preparations for going underground proved to have been quite inadequate, and although some cadres escaped abroad the capacity of the Party to act inside Germany virtually disappeared. But what was more serious as viewed from Moscow was the failure of Hitler's non-Nazi backers to exercise the expected control over him. Events showed that they had most seriously underestimated the skill, ruthlessness and dynamism of Hitler as a political leader, and that not they, but Hitler, was henceforth going to decide German foreign policy.

In retrospect it was clear that it would have been far better both for the German Communists and for the Soviet Union if a *bloc* of all Left and Centre forces in Germany had been formed to keep Hitler out of power. This conclusion was inevitably drawn by those disillusioned Stalinists who, as we have seen,[1] sought a relaxation from the intolerable strains imposed on Russian internal affairs by Stalin's policies and took steps at the 'Congress of Victors' to curb his power. This was the brief 'liberal spell' which intervened in the history of the CPSU from the autumn of 1933 to the summer of 1936, between the rigours of the Five-year Plan and the fury of the Great Purge. Not that it was really 'liberal' by any Western standards, but it could be called so in comparison with what preceded and followed it. In the field of Comintern affairs this period was reflected in a new policy – that of the Popular Front. The Communists abroad were now to march under the banner of 'anti-Fascism'; instead of

1. Chapter 10, p. 108.

holding aloof from other parties of the Left and concentrating their political activity on denouncing and vilifying them, the Communists were to offer their co-operation for preserving democratic liberties and averting Fascist dictatorships. The country most immediately concerned was France, where the riots organized in the Place de la Concorde on 6 February 1934 by groups of the extreme Right brought down the Daladier Cabinet and seemed to be the prelude to a dictatorship on the model of those already ruling in Rome and Berlin. The scare was not in fact well grounded, for six decades of the politics of the Third Republic had given democracy in France a degree of immunity to the Fascist virus which it had never possessed in Italy or Germany, and the career of Colonel de la Rocque as a would-be Fascist dictator was as much of a fiasco as that of Sir Oswald Mosley in Britain. But it was natural, in view of what had so recently happened in Germany, that the threat of Fascism in France should be taken seriously by those most likely to suffer from it. The French Communist Party, which had always been a rather unruly one as seen from Moscow, now split over the policy to be pursued; the faithful Thorez, *fils du peuple*, stood fast on the Left extremist line until ordered to change it, while the fiery Doriot, acting on his own initiative, urged an alliance with the Socialists to combat the Fascist danger. He was expelled from the Party for disobedience,[2] and the Party then, on instructions from Moscow, adopted the policy he had advocated. It had been decided within the CPSU that the Comintern line was to be changed. The Paris riots of 6 February had occurred while the Seventeenth Congress of the CPSU was still actually in session, and the months that followed were the heyday of the liberal spell inside the Soviet Union. After deliberations in the Politburo the faithful Thorez was

2. Doriot became a lone wolf in French left-wing politics and finally a collaborator with the Germans in 1940–45.

told to make a pact with the Socialists and he did. The pact was soon afterwards extended to the bourgeois Radicals, and the Popular Front came into being.

The Communists now changed their slogans. During the period of Left extremism they had on every possible occasion shouted 'Les Soviets partout', expressing their will to make a proletarian revolution on the Russian model if they ever had the chance. Now the slogans were 'For labour, liberty and peace' or 'Against Fascism and war'. The enthusiasm for democracy was quite new and the Communists needed a little time to get used to it. The ardour for peace, on the other hand, had existed among the French Communists from the beginning, but the word now acquired quite a new meaning. It had signified an uncompromising opposition to every form of the military power of a bourgeois state – the army, military conscription, armaments and taxes for the up-keep of the forces – and even more to any war which might conceivably be waged by such a state. The Communists were not alone in France in such an attitude; in the wake of the First World War, in which she had lost more men than any other belligerent in proportion to her population,[3] an intense emotional pacifism had spread through France; it was dominant among the Socialists and deeply affected the Radicals. It expressed itself in a resolve that France should never go to war again if it could possibly be avoided and in hostility to army officers, armament manufacturers and 'Poincaré la Guerre'. The Communists did all they could to exploit and exacerbate these sentiments. But now something else was required, for the Soviet Union, disappointed in its hopes of a military alliance with Germany, was seeking one with France against Germany. 'Peace', therefore, now meant French Communist support for the French army and for a programme of rearmament to defend the *status*

3. Certainly more than Germany or Britain; it is possible that Russian casualties were relatively even heavier, but there are no reliable figures for them.

quo established in Europe by the Treaty of Versailles. The new interpretation was given authoritatively by a public statement that 'Stalin understands and supports unreservedly the policy of national defence followed by France so as to maintain her armed forces on the level necessary to maintain security'.

This announcement was naturally far more welcome on the Right of French politics and in military circles than among the pacifists of the Left who were not subject to Communist Party discipline and found difficulty in changing their most fundamental beliefs overnight. Thus arose a paradoxical situation in which the French Communists were linked with the parties of the Left – the Socialists and Radicals – in an electoral coalition, but on defence and foreign policy were nearer to that section of the French Right which continued to follow the hard-line policy towards Germany inherited from Clemenceau, Poincaré and Tardieu. For the time being the tactic of being on the Left and on the Right at the same time was very successful. At the Fête Nationale on 14 July 1935 Thorez appeared together with Blum and Daladier at a vast demonstration in the Place de la Bastille for the defence of the Republic against Colonel de la Rocque. But the Right, apart from the Colonel's insignificant following, noted with satisfaction that the Communists had now become patriotic Frenchmen ready to endorse rearmament and the promotion of French national interests in Europe. Nor was the satisfaction cancelled at that time by any fear that the Popular Front would subvert the social order, for the Radicals, who, although sometimes a nuisance to the *haute bourgeoisie*, were deeply devoted to private property, could be relied on to prevent their proletarian partners from striking any serious blow at the capitalist system.

This agreeable state of affairs lasted until 26 May 1936. The Popular Front, with the Radicals, Socialists and Communists combining for second-ballot voting, brought great electoral successes, first in the municipal elections of June 1935 and then in the parliamentary general election of April 1936, which gave the three parties together a majority in the Chamber: Blum, the leader of the Socialists, became Prime Minister and took office on 5 June; the Communists declined to participate in the new government, but promised it the support of their votes in the Chamber.

But even before Blum took office, an event occurred which was entirely unexpected and took both the Socialists and the Communists by surprise. On 26 May and the two following days the workers in the aircraft industry went on strike and occupied the factories; this was followed by strikes in one industry after another in a kind of tidal wave of militant working-class action. The strike movement was not promoted by any political party; it was inspired by the anarcho-syndicalist tradition which had been strong among the French workers from the late nineteenth century and glorified the strike as the mode of action appropriate for the working class in all its dealings with capitalist employers. France was involved in a financial crisis and there was an accumulation of workers' grievances; the advent of a Socialist government raised hopes that the state would this time be on the side of the workers, and once the strike movement had begun and had had initial successes, it spread like wildfire. The intention was not revolutionary in the sense that there was any purpose of capturing the state, but the movement had a revolutionary edge to it in so far as the occupation of the factories was a direct challenge to the legal property rights of the bourgeoisie – as a mere withholding of labour was not. The success of the strikes was phenomenal; the employers, utterly dismayed at their vast scale and unable to call on a Socialist government for the kind of intervention which they might have expected from one of the Right, capitulated and on 7 June signed the famous Matignon Agreement, which conceded practically all the workers' demands, including large wage increases, recognized status for trade unions and shop stewards, a forty-hour week and holidays with pay. Parts of the Agreement were written into law by legislation which was passed through the Chamber and Senate almost without opposition. Superficially a great victory had been won by the French proletariat without bloodshed and the outcome had been accepted by the bourgeoisie. But the strikes, and particularly the occupations of the factories, had created an intense alarm and resentment on the Right. Inevitably the Communists were blamed for the outbreak. In fact they had not initiated it, but, as it gained momentum, they tried to take over the leadership of it so as to establish themselves as the champions of the workers at the expense of both the Socialists and the syndicalists. As a result the Communists increased their working-class following, but in so doing they came to be regarded by the French middle classes as a really dangerous revolutionary force and to inspire a fear and hatred which they could not have evoked in their days of impotent Left extremism.

A profound social and political division in France must have been a consequence of the great strike wave of May 1936, but it was sharply accentuated by the outbreak of civil war in Spain in July. All France took sides in the war and sympathies on each side were inflamed by reports of the atrocities which from the outset were committed by both sides in the ferocious struggle destined to devour Spain for nearly three years. France itself was close to civil war; in order to avoid it Blum adopted the policy of official non-intervention in the war, but he could not stop the envenomed controversy from dividing France as nothing had divided it since the *affaire Dreyfus*.

The Spanish civil war was as unexpected for the directors of the Comintern in Moscow as the May strikes in France had been a few weeks earlier. For some time it seems that Stalin could not make up his mind what course to pursue. But in Spain, as in France, while certainly not unaware that patronage of revolutionary forces would endanger the Franco–Russian alliance, he finally acted on the principle that he could not afford to repudiate an effectively militant proletarian movement in Western Europe because to do so would be to abandon his claim to worldwide leadership of the working class to the Socialists and the anarcho-syndicalists. The Spanish situation was, of course, far more critical for him than the affair of the French strikes, because it involved not merely the attitude of local Communists but a commitment of the Soviet Union itself in the international arena. The intervention in Spain on which he ultimately decided was conducted within very narrow limits; it was never comparable in scale or vigour with the interventions of Germany and Italy on the side of Franco, but it was sufficient to save Madrid in the autumn of 1936 and keep the war going until the collapse of the Republic at the beginning of 1939. Some Red Army officers were sent to give technical assistance and training to the Republican forces, but were told to 'keep out of range of artillery fire'; the fighting force of the intervention was provided by non-Soviet Communists, largely exiles from Italy and Germany, who were recruited into the International Brigades and sent to Spain as volunteers. War material, which the Republicans could neither produce for themselves nor obtain from France or Britain, was provided by the Soviet Union, but it was not only paid for from the Spanish national gold reserve which was conveyed from Spain to Odessa for the purpose; it was also used by Stalin for political leverage to ensure for the Spanish Communists a pre-eminent political position in the Republic to which their following in Spain – they had been of far less importance than the Socialists or Anarchists before the civil war – did not entitle them. This policy promised a political advantage whichever way the war went. If the Republic were victorious, it would be under Communist leadership; if Franco won, they could still claim the principal credit for a heroic resistance.

There was, however, a price which had to be paid. The antagonism of the French Right towards Communism and the Soviet Union became so great that it invalidated not only the Franco–Soviet Pact but also the French alliance with Czechoslovakia which had been underwritten by the Soviet Union. The French Right, with few exceptions, became converts to the doctrine of appeasement. Hitler might be a tough customer, but he was preferable to the deluge of Soviet-inspired proletarian revolution which could now be anticipated as the consequence of his overthrow. By the autumn of 1938 enormous opposition had developed in France to fulfilment of the alliance commitment to Czechoslovakia; the intervention of Britain provided the French Government – by that time no longer a genuine Popular Front Government, but a Radical one relying on votes well to the right of the Popular Front majority in the Chamber – with an excuse for inaction, but it would in any case have then been impossible to take France into the war as a united nation. Stalin no longer had France as an ally. Fortunately for him he soon found a substitute. When Britain in March 1939 reversed her foreign policy and gave a guarantee to Poland, Hitler found it expedient to bid for his friendship. For a country in which all active Communists had been put to death or imprisoned, there could be no risk in a pact with the Kremlin.

13. Communism and the Second World War

Russia was closely involved in the origins of the Second World War as she was in those of the First, but the fact that she had in the meantime become a state dedicated to the Communist ideology made a difference to the character of the involvement. In the period from 1934 to 1939 the Soviet Union in its public official policy and in its propaganda directed to liberal democratic circles in Western countries had adopted the political line of 'anti-Fascism' and support for 'collective security' through the League of Nations. The movement of Soviet policy towards alignment with the Western democracies and the League, which had previously been the target of the fiercest Communist denunciation, had the effect of producing an ever-increasing sympathy and respect for the Soviet Union in quarters which had hitherto been deeply hostile or suspicious; the Communists internally as well as internationally became respectable, acquiring the reputation of being the purest of patriots and the most ardent of democrats. In France, as we have seen, this reputation was largely destroyed by the Communist involvement in the semi-revolutionary occupation of factories in France in May and June of 1936, and the revolutionary regime created by armed workers in Madrid and Barcelona in July of the same year after Franco's revolt had made the Popular Front Government of Spain dependent on proletarian para-military forces. But in Britain, where there was no threat of revolution, the adversaries of 'appeasement' continued to have faith in Russia and to call for an alliance in order to 'stop Hitler'. The policy of appeasement itself, as pursued by the British Government under Baldwin and Chamberlain, was due more to traditional isolationism and the hope of keeping out of the troubles of Europe than to the active hostility towards Russia which prevailed on the Right in French politics, but there was certainly a strong distaste for a close alliance with a power with which there were so few channels of contact and understanding, even if the difference of ideology were to be entirely ignored. When, nevertheless, Britain reversed the policy of appeasement after Hitler's march into Prague and gave a guarantee of protection to Poland at the end of March 1939, a rather half-hearted attempt was made to obtain a Russian alliance. But the very fact that Britain had guaranteed Poland made Hitler for the first time interested in a return to the policy of a Russo-German alliance against Poland which had been favoured by the Reichswehr in the time of the Weimar Republic. Once he had entered the auction Hitler had no difficulty in outbidding Britain, for he could offer Stalin a partition of the independent countries of Eastern Europe between Germany and the Soviet Union, whereas Britain and France could only offer commitment to a war of which the Soviet Union would inevitably bear the brunt without any promises of territorial aggrandizement.

The secret partition pact which accompanied the public Treaty of Non-aggression between the Soviet Union and Germany was an agreement between two aggressive powers in the most cynical tradition of *Realpolitik*; it resembled the agreement about Poland once made between Frederick of Prussia and the Tsarina Catherine, and would undoubtedly have received the admiring approval of both those monarchs if their spirits could have been raised from the dead in order to give an opinion on it. But how was such a deal to be justified in terms of collective security, anti-Fascism, the Popular Fronts and the campaign for 'peace and democracy'? How was this behaviour to be represented as appropriate to the image of the Soviet regime formed for Western public opinion by such writers as Sydney and Beatrice Webb, John Strachey and Harold Laski? In the last resort Stalin did not care if large numbers of liberal and socialist fellow-travellers or pro-Soviet sympathizers were shocked and disillusioned by the Nazi–Soviet Pact; they were in any case an unreliable and expendable element, and the Popular Front and League of Nations tactics which had won their support had already served their purpose. It was a more serious consideration that there were many in the Communist parties themselves who were unable to swallow a pact with Hitler for the conquest and partition of neighbouring states. A considerable effort was therefore made to justify the policy. Great emphasis was laid on the reluctance of Britain and France to make a firm alliance with Russia; this, it was claimed, had forced Stalin into an agreement with Germany as the only way of ensuring the security of the Soviet Union, to which both the Soviet Government itself and Communists in other countries ought to give the highest priority. At the same time the secret partition agreement was kept a secret, and the moves made by the Soviet Union in accordance with it were skilfully represented as improvised responses to the German aggression against Poland. Soviet troops did not move into Poland until a large part of the country had been overrun by the Germans, and Stalin could claim that he was merely taking over a portion of Polish territory to stop the German army from coming right up to the Soviet frontier. Soviet moves into the Baltic states were justified on the same ground. Any suggestion of collusion or prearrangement with Nazi Germany was strongly denied, and there was no proof of it until German documents relating to it, which were captured by the Americans in Germany in 1945, were later published by them after the breakdown of the Soviet–U S war-time alliance.

The way had been cleared for a Russo–German alliance against Poland as early as 1937 by the dissolution of the Polish Communist Party by order of the Comintern.

This was a unique case; Poland was the only country in the world which was thus deprived of the privilege of possessing a Communist Party of its own and it was thereby de-recognized as a national state. A Polish Communist Party, however devoted to the international Communist cause, could not be trusted to refrain from protest if Polish national independence were to be wiped out by agreement between the Soviet Union and Nazi Germany; such a protest would be highly embarrassing, and the best and simplest way to forestall the danger was to abolish the Polish Party as a unit of the international movement. Later on a new Polish Party was to be formed by fiat of Stalin, but it would be entirely Soviet-based and would be put in power in Poland by the Soviet armed forces at war with Germany; because of this notorious later collaboration between Stalin and the Polish Communists (or 'Workers' Party' as they were called in their new incarnation), the earlier suppression of the party was forgotten and indeed appears to have escaped the notice of most of the historians who have dealt with the origins of the Second World War; it provides very strong confirmation of the allegation of the defecting Soviet intelligence agent Walter Krivitsky that already in 1937 Stalin was aiming at an agreement with Hitler and that alliances with the Western powers against Germany were for him never more than a *pis aller*. From his point of view no question of Marxist-Leninist principle was involved; he had no real preference for bourgeois democracy as against Fascism, which would indeed hardly have been possible for a man who aimed at an unlimited personal despotism. He had come to identify completely the worldwide cause of Communism with the state interest of the Soviet Union, and therefore to extend the boundaries of the Soviet Union and increase its strategic security without fighting a war was the best thing he could do both for his country and for the Communist cause. If his conduct seemed to so many at the time outrageously cynical and treacherous, it was because they had mistaken the tactical slogans of the Popular Front period for something permanent and fundamental and had failed to realize that the Party line for that period was merely one of temporary expediency.

When the European war had begun with the Soviet Union as an ally of Germany against Poland, but a neutral in relation to the war of Germany, Britain and France, a distinction had to be drawn in Communist propaganda between the justifiable invasions of Poland and Finland by the Soviet Union and the unjustifiable imperialist war being waged (not at first very vigorously) between the Great Powers of Western Europe. Since Britain and France were not allied with the Soviet Union in their war against Germany on behalf of Poland, it followed that it was an imperialist war which no Communist could support. Actually, the Communists of the West were given no line from Moscow for more than a fortnight after the German invasion of Poland and were allowed to support the Anglo–French war effort until the Soviet Union's own invasion of Poland; this delay was necessary in order to conceal the fact that a partition of Poland had been prearranged between Moscow and Berlin. But once the partition had been completed the Communists were ordered to oppose any further continuation of the war. It was certainly in Stalin's interest that the war should end as soon as he had gathered his winnings from the deal with Hitler. If the war did not go on, peace would have to be made on the basis of the *fait accompli* in Eastern Europe and recognition of the territorial acquisitions made by both Germany and Russia. At this time it is very unlikely that Stalin was preoccupied with fear of a German victory if the war continued; his apprehension must have been rather that the war might spread to the Mediterranean and the Balkans or Scandinavia and involve Russia in hostilities with Britain and France. Britain had guaranteed Greece and Rumania, and concluded an alliance with Turkey – a combination which carried a potential threat to the Soviet Union in its two most vulnerable sectors, the Ukraine and the Caucasus. There was also the possibility of an Anglo-French intervention to help Finland. The military prestige of France was still unimpaired and nobody anticipated the total collapse of France which was shortly to take place.

When it did take place Stalin hurried to complete his control of the areas assigned to the Soviet Union by the secret treaty with Germany and tried to contest diplomatically an exclusive ascendancy of Germany in the Balkans, but he appears not to have expected a German attack on Russia and his disbelief became a fixed idea immune to contrary evidence, so that he was taken by surprise when it happened. His refusal to give credence to reports, whether from British sources or from his own intelligence service, was due not to any faith in Hitler's goodwill but to a calculation that it would be too risky for him to attack Russia while still at war with England and that Hitler would think so too. A merciless bully towards the weak, Stalin was nevertheless by temperament very cautious when confronted with power comparable to his own, and he would certainly never have done what Hitler did in June 1941. He fatally underestimated the inflation of Hitler's self-confidence after the fall of France and his propensity to play *va banque*. Stalin made up his mind that Hitler would not attack and thereafter rejected all evidence of his intention as misinformation fed into intelligence channels either by the British in order to stir up trouble between Russia and Germany or by the Germans themselves in order to put pressure behind their diplomacy. When the German army did attack, therefore, it achieved full strategic surprise and the war began with a series of great German victories.

From the day when Hitler's armed forces crossed the Soviet frontier, Britain's cause against Germany ceased for the Communists to be an imperialist war and became a crusade against Fascism. The Russo–German war involved an immediate return to the slogans and tactics of the Popular Front period. Communists in Britain and the United States became once more democrats and patriots, and instead of urging that Britain should make peace with Hitler (and that the United States should refrain from helping Britain to wage war) became the most bellicose of anti-Nazis ready to bring accusations of pusillanimity and even of Fascist sympathies against anyone who doubted the wisdom of early seaborne landings on the European continent in order to create a 'Second Front' and relieve the military pressure on Russia. From the side of the British Government Churchill had no hesitation in publicly assuring Russia of full British support in a common cause against Hitler's Germany; his former detestation of what he had once called 'the foul baboonery of Bolshevism' was now forgotten in his determination to overcome and eliminate the threat of a German hegemony of Europe.

Stalin as autocratic ruler of the Soviet Union and leader of all Communists throughout the world had two aims in the war. The first was to ensure the survival of the Soviet Union and for that end to make all possible use of military alliances, using the Communists abroad to reinforce and stimulate the war efforts of his allies. The second was to regain after the war by agreement with his new allies the territories he had obtained in Eastern Europe by the deal with Hitler and to extend, if possible, the Soviet frontiers even further westward, while at the same time bringing the nations to the east of Germany and Italy under a predominant Soviet influence and control in the event of a decisive Allied victory in the war. In this latter task foreign Communists would have two functions to perform. Those in the areas to be brought under Soviet control must first assist the Soviet forces in the struggle against Germany; they would then be put into power in their respective countries by Soviet military backing and would thereafter be required to govern as vassals of Stalin under the supervision of Soviet power. For Communists outside the zone of prospective Soviet military occupation, and particularly in Britain and the U S, the assigned function was to be to carry on propaganda to justify the Soviet expansion in Eastern Europe, to vilify and discredit anit-Communist political elements there, and to oppose any policies which might thwart or obstruct the accomplishment of Stalin's purpose.

The political success of Communism from June 1941 to the unconditional surrender of Germany in May 1945 was indeed remarkable. It could not, of course, have been gained without the military victories which were won by Russian arms. But these victories, however welcome to Allied nations and however productive of respect for Russian power, could not have created in the West an image of Stalin's regime as a benevolent, peace-loving and freedom-loving state had they not been thus turned to account by a skilful, persistent and highly organized propaganda. The advantage which the Communists enjoyed during these years of war was that it was virtually impossible to object to their propaganda or to criticize the 'Soviet myth' which it projected because any opposition to it incurred suspicion of pro-German sympathies or of reversion to the discredited spirit of appeasement. It was almost a defection to the enemy if anyone in Britain or the U S suggested that Stalin was a ruthless tyrant or that the Poles had just cause for grievance against Russia. Since Russia was an ally, and an ally without whom the war could not be won, it was essential to avoid saying anything which might cause unpleasantness, and since one could only speak favourably of Russia it was psychologically convenient to believe what one said. The tendency to indulge in euphemism about Russia, to whitewash Stalin and give him the benefit of every doubt prevailed at all levels of politics and publicity. It applied above all to the Moscow trials and the 'confessions' produced at them; the British Ambassador in Moscow used to repeat on all possible occasions his favourite epigram that 'the Russians had no fifth column because they had shot them all', and Churchill eagerly and uncritically swallowed the story told him by Beneš (who had himself been misled by information planted by Skoblin) that Stalin had wiped out a majority of the generals of the Red Army because they were pro-German. Churchill, however, always retained a certain mistrust of Stalin and an idea that Communism could be dangerous to British interests if it were to prevail in such a country as Greece. He was prepared to deal with Stalin in an old-fashioned way on a basis of spheres of influence and to assent to a large-scale Soviet expansion in Eastern Europe provided Stalin would give Britain a free hand in Greece. The attitude of Roosevelt was different in that he really seems to have taken seriously his notions of the Four Freedoms and the Four Policemen and to have imagined that Stalin would be willing to co-operate with him in building a world of independent democratic nations. In practice the difference between the attitudes of the two Western statesmen did not matter very much as long as the war was not yet won; both of them agreed at Yalta to a solution of the 'Polish problem' providing for withdrawal of *de jure* recognition of the Polish Government in Exile which had led the Polish nation in war against Germany for five years and its transfer to a 'broadened' version of the Communist regime imposed on Poland by the Soviet forces of military occupation. It was only after Germany was finally beaten that the difference between the British and US attitudes became really important; Churchill then wanted US support in opposing a further extension of Soviet power in Europe, but the US government, which remained Rooseveltian in its outlook for some time after the death of Roosevelt himself, saw no reason to provide it.

Stalin showed great political skill in persuading the Western governments that he was only interested in security for his country and had no desire to spread Communism. On 22 May 1943 as a gesture to Britain and the United States he proclaimed the dissolution of the Comintern; it was an act without real meaning, for the international organization of Communist parties, which had long since been nothing more than an extension of the apparatus of the CPSU, remained intact as an instrument of Kremlin policy, but it certainly had the desired effect in the West; it was taken as a final confirmation of Stalin's well-known policy of 'socialism in one country' and proof that it would in future be possible to deal with the Soviet Union as with any other nation state, free from fears of revolutionary subversion across national frontiers. But those who believed that the dissolution of the Comintern meant that the Soviet Union would no longer seek to promote Communist power abroad were destined to a rude awakening after the war was over – or indeed even before it was finished. In spite of measures taken to conceal Communist seizures of power under cover of multi-party coalitions it gradually became evident that the advance of the Soviet armies was being used politically to set up Communist-controlled governments. These were 'revolutions from above' in the sense that they were not achieved by movements of popular insurrection, but depended on the backing of overwhelmingly strong military forces coming in from outside. The only part of Europe where the Communists as a result of war-time conditions became strong enough to win power on their own, without dependence on Soviet arms, was the western Balkans – Yugoslavia, Albania and Greece. Neither in Poland, Rumania, Bulgaria, Hungary or the Soviet occupation zone of Germany could they have captured power by themselves; even in Czechoslovakia, where they took over by a *coup de force* two years after the end of the war without the direct intervention of Soviet troops, the threat of such intervention was a major factor in deterring resistance to the *coup*. As a result of the war eight new Communist states in addition to the Soviet Union emerged in Europe, and only two of them – Yugoslavia and Albania – could be claimed as primarily products of domestic political developments. The others were creations of Russian military power reaching out westward in victorious campaigns to Budapest, Prague and Berlin.

14. Communism and the Cold War

Seven and a half years elapsed between the unconditional surrender of Japan, which terminated the Second World War in August 1945, and the death of Stalin in March 1953. During those years, for the world at large, Stalin was Communism and Communism was Stalin – even though a crack appeared in the 'monolithic' edifice when Communist Yugoslavia defied Stalin's authority from 1947 onwards. The Soviet Union, after having suffered enormous human losses during the war and having come near to collapse in the bitter campaigns of 1941 and 1942, had emerged from the struggle as the strongest single power in Europe and Asia and the strongest power in the world but for the United States. The only effective curb on the exercise of Stalin's authority in Europe and Asia was one which would be imposed by the United States, and whether they would try to impose such a curb depended on US presidential policy and the climate of US public opinion. During the war Roosevelt, with his faith in Stalin's good intentions as a would-be maker of a peaceful and democratic world, took no steps to place obstacles in the path of Soviet expansion, and US opinion was swayed by enthusiasm and admiration for Russia as an effective fighting ally – a mood secured for the time being against doubts and suspicions by a war-time censorship which suppressed all news adverse to Stalin's image. But this state of affairs began to change soon after Roosevelt's death. His successor was a man of a different mental outlook – more of a realist in politics and less disposed to take seriously the kind of meaningless verbiage which had come out of the Teheran and Yalta conferences. He was not interested in grandiose visions of world government by the 'Big Three' on the assumption that they would always be acting in friendly co-operation; he was concerned with what the Russians under Stalin's supreme authority were actually doing in Europe and Asia and he found their actions provocative and alarming. He did not alter U S policy at once on taking over the Presidency; partly because he was inexperienced in foreign affairs and unprepared for taking major decisions, partly because his military advisers insisted that nothing be done which might offend Russia while the war with Japan was still unfinished, and partly because public opinion, conditioned during the war to a strongly pro-Soviet attitude, took time to get accustomed to the idea that it might become a political necessity for the U S to 'contain' Russia. After the end of the war with Japan, however, President Truman's policy became more and more one of opposition to Russian expansion, and this trend had increasingly the support of U S public opinion.

Later on there was much argument in retrospect on the question who started what came to be known as 'the cold war'. The Communists, both officially in the Communist-ruled countries, and unofficially in non-Communist countries, held that Russia and the U S had been amicably co-operating while Roosevelt was President, and that Russia had desired to continue this co-operation, but that the friendship had been destroyed by Truman acting under the influence of 'Wall Street imperialism'. What happened was indeed that U S policy changed; it changed from one of acquiescence to one of opposition in relation to Russia's European expansion. Soviet–U S friendship meant that the U S would allow the Soviet Union to do as it pleased in Europe; as soon as the U S government began trying to check the advance of Soviet power, the friendship was inevitably marred. At Yalta Roosevelt told Stalin that the U S would not keep occupation troops in Germany for more than two years after the end of the war; certainly he had no idea of using the

US army to prevent Stalin from taking over the Western sectors of Berlin or the Western occupation zones of Germany. Had all US troops been withdrawn from Germany in 1947, as Roosevelt had told Stalin that they would be, the German Communists with Soviet military backing would certainly have been able to take over control of Western as well as of Eastern Germany; neither Britain nor France would then have been strong enough to take the risk of a military confrontation with the Soviet Union. It was therefore a great disappointment to Stalin when the US, instead of removing her forces from Europe and leaving the field clear for Russia, remained both in West Germany and in West Berlin, compelling him to choose between setting a limit to his advance or embarking on a major war. Soviet policy thereafter had one supreme aim – to get the Americans out of Europe. 'Americans, go home!' – or, with somewhat less grammatical use of the English language, 'Americans go America!' – was the slogan chalked or painted by the French Communists on every wall where a US soldier might be expected to see it in the years after 1947; but they did not go, and with the conclusion of the North Atlantic Alliance as a response to the Russian blockade of Berlin their presence in Europe became permanent.

It is difficult to give a historical account of Stalin's designs and calculations in foreign policy during this period because Stalin took his decisions in secret, sometimes in consultation with a group of chosen advisers – not necessarily the Politburo – and sometimes without consulting anyone at all. There can be no doubt that he possessed supreme autocratic power in the Soviet Union after the completion of the Great Purge in 1938 and that nobody else would have dared to take important steps in the field of foreign affairs without his approval. It is therefore from Soviet actions and from the actions of those foreign Communist parties which were most dependent on and subservient to the Soviet Union –

among whom were certainly to be reckoned the German Communists – that Stalin's policy has to be inferred. In this context the Soviet-supported endeavours of the German Communists to extend their 'Socialist Unity Party' to the Western zone of Germany and the Soviet attempt to gain control of West Berlin by resort to blockade indicate a will to 'satellize' Germany and bring it into the system to which Poland, Hungary and Czechoslovakia already belonged. The German Question was indeed primary and fundamental for Soviet policy. Control of Germany would mean an effective Soviet hegemony in Europe, for, if Communist rule were to be extended to the Rhine, France, where as a result of the war the Right was for the time being discredited and more than a quarter of the electorate was voting Communist, would soon have to fall into line. For Stalin by 1945 the interests of Russia as an imperial state had become identical with the cause of Communism. Soviet power could be used to impose Communism on a conquered or intimidated country and Communist parties could be used to support and consolidate Soviet power. Where there were Soviet military forces, accompanied by armed security police units, as in Poland, Rumania and Hungary, Communist parties could be put in power, however small and weak they had previously been; even when Soviet troops were no longer actually in occupation, as in Czechoslovakia in 1948, the Communists could be helped to power by a threat of Soviet military intervention. It was assumed that these parties, so dependent on Soviet support for rule over peoples who would never have given them power but for the presence of the Soviet army, would in their own interest, if not from ideological conviction, be the faithful vassals of their suzerain lord in Moscow, and so indeed they were as long as Stalin lived, with the exception of Yugoslavia, which was the exception to prove the rule, for Yugoslavia was the only country where the Communists came to power mainly through their own efforts in the war-time resistance to

German conquest and not simply because of the Russian military advance.

The regimes set up by Stalin in the countries overrun by the Russian armies were not in form pure single-party dictatorships as in the Soviet Union but coalitions in which the non-Communist elements accepted the 'leadership' of the Communists. They styled themselves 'People's Democracies' and their claim to rest on a broad political base echoed the language and sentiments of the Popular Fronts of the late thirties. The purpose of these arrangements was partly to mitigate the unfavourable impression produced in the West by Communist takeovers, and partly to provide a cover under which non-Communist politicians who were willing to be employed might be enlisted for administrative tasks without being given any real share in political power. Among those who served in the non-Communist stooge parties there were a few who, either from faith in Communist assurances or from confidence in their own skill, hoped to participate in the making of policy, but they were soon disillusioned by their experience of working with the Communists; the majority never expected to be more than puppets politically, but sought jobs and privileges for themselves and their families at a time when there was widespread distress and destitution for all classes in the wake of the war. Apart from these 'collaborators' the Communist rulers had very little support except in Yugoslavia where they had headed a national movement. They had too obviously been put in power by foreign conquerors, and those who put them in power – the Soviet military and police forces – had not made themselves loved in the territories they occupied. In Germany, Austria, Hungary and Rumania the Russians had come as enemies and avengers settling accounts for the invasion of the Soviet Union by Hitler and his allies; even in Poland and Czechoslovakia, where the Russians were theoretically liberators of their own allies, their behaviour was decidedly rough. Their excesses did nothing to increase the attractions of the ideology which they professed; the 'New Soviet Man', hailed by Communist propaganda as the morally superior product of a social system purged of bourgeois selfishness, seemed remarkably similar to the Old Adam in the experience of those who suffered from his propensities for pillage and rape. But if the Russians failed to win affection, they certainly inspired fear; they appeared irresistible and there was no appeal or redress against their arbitrary actions. People who protested were liable to find themselves deported to a forced labour camp beyond the Volga. Throughout Eastern Europe, as in Germany, sensible folk had learned in recent years to keep their mouths shut and stay on the right side of authority. 'O God, make me dumb and keep me out of Dachau!' had been the good German's prayer under the Nazi regime; it was the same in the Soviet zone in 1946 except that Kolyma was substituted for Dachau. The new system of Communist power organized by Stalin was built on apathy and resignation, on submission to overwhelming force and the absence of any practical alternative; it lacked the wide and ardent popular support which the Russian Bolsheviks had been able to muster in 1917 and which the Yugoslav and Chinese Communists could command in 1945. It was revolution from outside and from above, not from within and from below.

In principle there could be no limit to the policy of extending the boundaries of Communism by the power of the Red Army. If it was right and proper to use Soviet occupation forces to put Communists in power in Warsaw or Budapest, it would have been just as right and proper to do it in Paris or Rome. Indeed Stalin in his later correspondence with Tito over the disputes which finally produced the rupture between Yugoslavia and the Soviet Union claimed that the Soviet Union by driving out the Germans from Belgrade and Zagreb had 'created the conditions for the Yugoslav Communists to take power', but had 'unfortunately' been unable to do the same for the French or Italian Communists. This inability was not necessarily final; if the U S would only withdraw from Europe, Stalin might still find opportunities for intervention in the affairs of France and Italy. But this was not to be in Stalin's lifetime, for by 1950 Western Europe had been consolidated both economically and militarily against further Soviet expansion; economically by the Marshall Plan and militarily by the North Atlantic Treaty which formally committed the U S to European defence.

The formation of N A T O, which had been preceded by the U S protection given to Greece and Turkey under the Truman Doctrine of 1947, set a limit to Soviet expansion, for no further move was now possible without a grave risk of war, and it was not a war that Stalin wanted. His policy was one requiring the use of force, but it was to be force against the weak, the defeated or the disunited, not against an adversary of equal or superior strength. Hitler, a good judge in such matters, once described Stalin as an 'ice-cold blackmailer', and with the coldness of his mind went caution and a very wary calculation of risks. Recklessness was no part of his character; he was not a man to be carried away by momentary anger. His way was to take everything he could get without undue risk, to exploit with the utmost cynicism the naïve generosity of a Roosevelt, but to draw back when confronted with a might and a will comparable to his own. His innate caution was demonstrated when the crisis came over the blockade of Berlin; he had believed – and so had Western diplomats insufficiently up to date in the technological possibilities of air transport – that West Berlin must be slowly strangled if all ground communications were cut off. But when it became clear that West Berlin could be kept alive by the air lift alone, Stalin was faced with the choice between acceptance of failure and extension of the blockade to the air by shooting down Western aircraft. In the event no aircraft were shot down and the conflict over Berlin was settled on terms which were a clear victory for the West.

This was the first great blow to Stalin's prestige; it cut him down to size after a period during which he had towered over Europe as a figure of more than human dimensions. No less damaging to his reputation as a superman was his failure to deal effectively with the defiance of Tito. The barrage of propaganda plus economic sanctions organized against Yugoslavia by the Soviet Union and the faithful satellites had no effect on the recalcitrants in Belgrade; a military punitive expedition was obviously called for to suppress the heretic and rebel within the Communist camp. That it was never launched was certainly not due to any moral scruples about the use of force against brother Communists; Tito was denounced in Soviet propaganda, accepted by official Communist parties throughout the world outside Yugoslavia as a Fascist and an agent of imperialism, and by Stalinist standards he deserved death no less than Zinoviev or Bukharin or Trotsky. But in view of the hostile confrontation between the Soviet *bloc* and the Western powers, Stalin could not be sure that, if he attacked Yugoslavia, he would not involve himself in a wider war. As in Berlin, he deemed discretion the better part of valour and he did not order the guns to fire.

The conflict between Russia and the West thus remained one of all tension short of war; the opposed armies did not move. The situation came to be known as 'the cold war' in contrast to a 'shooting war' or 'hot war'; nobody could regard it as peace, and yet it was not being fought with guns or bombs. The metaphor of frigidity was not indeed a very satisfactory one, because, if one wished to say that the situation was getting worse, one had to speak of its getting more icy, and correspondingly of any relaxation as a 'thaw', whereas increasing warmth should, to carry out the analogy, mean an approach to the 'hot' war which everyone feared. But, whatever the semantics involved, the fact was one of acute conflict and enmity between the two power *blocs* – those of East and West, as they came to be called. The tension was aggravated with the outbreak of the shooting war in Korea, in which the US was involved first against Communist North Korea and then against Communist China. There was no direct armed clash between the US and Russia, but Russia supplied war material to China and North Korea, and the US refrained from bombing or blockading Chinese territory for fear of Russian military intervention. The Korean war was still going on when Stalin died. This was an armed struggle by proxy, with the advantage to Russia that the Koreans, the Chinese and the nations which formed the United Nations expeditionary force in Korea all suffered heavy losses in three years of fighting while Russia did not lose a single soldier. Between the Soviet Union and the US, now recognized as the two 'superpowers' of the world, there was a strategic stalemate; neither was willing to go to war with the other and each was able to impose a limit on the other's actions. But they were divided by a mutual hostility which far exceeded the normal contentions of sovereign states in time of peace and there was no end in sight to their embittered rivalry.

15. Russian Communism after Stalin

The death of Stalin lifted from the Russian people a massive burden of fear which had weighed upon them for more than two decades. His had been a rule of terror, with the dreaded secret police watching and spying in every sector of Russian life. Set against the universal fear inspired by the purges and liquidations there was, however, an awed admiration for Stalin as the leader under whom Russia had acquired a powerful heavy industry and had emerged victorious from a desperately fought war. On the morrow of the entry of the Russian army into Berlin it is probable that feelings of admiration exceeded those of repulsion among the great majority of Russians. But by 1953 there was a general desire, both among the masses and in the Party itself, for a more relaxed way of living, and when the preliminary exposure of the 'Doctors' Plot' indicated that a great new purge was about to begin, alarm and despondency spread through all the population. In the midst of a growing anxiety about what the future was about to bring, Stalin had a cerebral haemorrhage and died.

'Destalinization' began almost immediately. The Doctors' Plot was declared to have been fabricated by the secret police. Since it implicated leading members of the Party, Stalin's successors could not do otherwise than declare the evidence to be false. But by so doing they discredited the secret police to a degree which could not but greatly reduce their status and power. Since the instrument was thus damaged, it became harder for anyone, however much he might wish to do so, to carry on the government by the methods Stalin had used. Moreover, after the terrible experience of the years since 1936, when nobody, however high his position in the Party, had been able to feel safe from arbitrary arrest and execution, there was a general desire among Party members to end autocracy and restore the oligarchic character of the party – 'collective leadership', it was called – as it had existed before Stalin established his system of personal rule.

In one way Stalin's very success in maintaining his tyranny had paved the way for a reversal of his system. He had put to death almost everyone in political life who had manifested independence of judgement, who had ever criticized or protested at anything he did. He had also suppressed by large-scale proscriptions and massacres all stirrings of nationalism in the non-Russian republics of the Union. Those who survived were the submissive and the obedient or the courtiers and sycophants who knew always how to keep on the right side of authority to their own personal advantage. It was therefore a very manageable Party and a very docile population that Stalin's successors in the Kremlin inherited from him. Terror was hardly necessary in order to keep control. New forces of political opposition might arise in the future, but in 1953 the peoples of the Soviet Union exhibited a cowed uniformity which made them governable with relatively little coercion. The new leaders could safely relax the rigours of the regime, and won popularity by doing so. The great danger for them was that one among their own number would try to grasp Stalin's sceptre and revive his despotism. The first aspirant was Beria, who had regained control of the secret police after Stalin's death – Stalin had demoted him in fear of his excessive power – and appears to have planned a *coup d'état*; he was trapped at a meeting of the Presidium and strangled by Malenkov and Mikoyan with the help of two army generals.[1] There was then a period of

1. Khrushchev gave this account to a leading Italian Communist; another version was that Beria was shot after a 'trial' by the Presidium.

genuine 'collective leadership', during which no single leader was outstanding. But by 1956 Khrushchev, who had been made First Secretary of the Party – the title of General Secretary which had been held by Stalin was not revived – had gathered a pre-eminent power into his hands; he had got rid of Malenkov as Prime Minister[2] and he was being built up in Press publicity by his henchmen in a way that suggested a hope of inheriting Stalin's mantle. To keep his ambition within bounds without repudiating his 'constitutional' leadership of the Party his colleagues decided that there must be a public (within the Party) exposure of Stalin's crimes and a formal denunciation of 'the cult of personality', which was supposed to have been the cause of them. A draft of a speech was prepared to be delivered to a closed session of the Twentieth Congress of the CPSU, and the Politburo called on Khrushchev to deliver it. He could not refuse, though there is reason to believe that he was extremely reluctant to give this 'Magna Carta' to the Party oligarchy.[3] Most of the facts brought out in the speech were already known to the delegates to the Congress, who had themselves lived under Stalin's terror, but it caused a sensation even among them to hear the truth about the formerly idolized 'Leader of Progressive Mankind' officially admitted by the First Secretary of the Party. The sensation in the world at large was even greater when the government of the United States, having obtained a copy of the speech from a foreign fraternal delegate present at the Congress, published it, so that everyone could read what Khrushchev had to say about his former master.

The speech had consequences quite unintended by its

2. 'People's Commissars' became 'Ministers' in 1946.

3. This interpretation is given by G. Paloczi-Horvath in *Khrushchev's Rise to Power*; see also B. Wolfe, *Khrushchev and Stalin's Ghost*. Khrushchev subsequently received the credit – in China discredit – for 'destalinization', but what evidence there is indicates that he was pushed into this course, proceeding on the principle of 'If you can't break 'em, join 'em'.

promoters, who had meant it only for the ears of members of the Party Congress and a few leading Communists from abroad. It had never been intended that the Party's dirty linen should be washed in the presence of a wider public, even of rank-and-file Communists, let alone one which would include critics and enemies of the Communist system. The effects of the speech were least within the Soviet Union itself, because it was there that the realities of Stalin's rule had been most fully known in spite of the officially propagated cult of his personality. It was outside Russia that ordinary Communists, fellow-travellers and sympathetic liberals had believed confidently in his wisdom and benevolence and had discounted the stories of his atrocities as inventions of malicious gossip. It was a terrible shock to all these people to find that their former idol had after all been guilty of the crimes of which he had been accused; it was even worse when they were derided by anti-Communists for having been taken in by a publicity which they now had to admit had been false. The prestige of Communism as such suffered a heavy blow. It was all very well to argue that the Stalin era now belonged to the past, and that everything in the Soviet Union was going to be quite different under the new leadership, but it was impossible that the image of Communism as a gospel for mankind should not be marred by the admission that the man who had guided its adherents over three decades had been a bloodthirsty monster. The demoralizing effect of Khrushchev's speech was very great among Communists abroad and was one of the causes of the upheavals which took place in Poland and Hungary later in the same year. Among Western liberals, on the other hand, after an initial consternation, the result was favourable to the Soviet regime, because it was widely believed that such a speech could not have been made without intentions of radical change in the Communist order, and there were even expectations of the gradual transformation of the regime into something like a liberal democracy. Khrushchev was built up as a heroic and enlightened reformer bravely struggling against a benighted Stalinist 'Old Guard'. This version was largely imaginary; the significant changes from Stalin's practice, in both domestic and foreign policies, had already been accomplished during the ascendancy of Malenkov, and little was added to destalinization by Khrushchev beyond the verbal denunciation of the dead dictator and the skilful political exploitation of his crimes against political opponents who had been somewhat more closely implicated in them than Krushchev himself had been. Khrushchev never had the slightest intention of introducing democracy into Russia. His slogan was a return to Leninism, and as it was Lenin who had suppressed all parties opposed to the Communists, it could not reasonably be expected that Russia would retrace its course to political liberty under this banner. For Party members destalinization simply meant that they could sleep soundly in their beds without keeping a suitcase ready packed to take to prison in case the police arrived in the middle of the night. It did not mean that the Party's monopoly of power was going to be abolished or that an opposition to Communism would be allowed to rear its ugly head.

The Central Committee of the Party resumed the authority it had had in Lenin's time and became a court of appeal against decisions of the Politburo. The First Secretary of the Party was in a position to pack the Central Committee both by his power to pick delegates to the Party Congress which elected the Committee and by his appointment of lower-grade Party Secretaries who were *ex officio* members of it. Thus Khrushchev was able not only to depose Malenkov from the office of Prime Minister early in 1955, but to crush in the summer of 1957 the 'anti-Party group', a faction formed by Malenkov with other malcontents to oust Khrushchev from the Party leadership. But in the autumn of 1964 the Central Committee turned against Khrushchev and deposed him.

His offence was his failure properly to represent the interests of those to whom he owed his power. Like Stalin, he had built himself up with the Party 'apparatus' as his foundation – the whole-time professional organizers and propagandists of the Party as distinct from the officials of the State bureaucracy. But also like Stalin he had in the end taken over in addition to his post as First Secretary of the Party the office of Prime Minister, so that he became both leader of the Party and head of the government. The Party leader who thus combines the two offices concentrates the maximum of power in his hands, but he still has to make up his mind which office he regards as the more important, and the question is a very practical one, because it involves the relative status and competence of Party and state officials. It is a theoretical issue also because it concerns the relation between the Party and the state in a Communist political system. The fundamental principle is that the Party directs the state and lays down the main lines of policy which the state then carries out. It may be thought that this principle is adequately put into effect if the state Ministers are Party members and if the most important decisions are taken by the Party's Politburo (some or all of whose members also hold state offices). But the Party has an existence separate from the state; it has its own organization and its own bureaucracy of full-time professionals. It is these people, the *apparatchiki*, who are the hard core of the Party; it is they who are the special guardians and beneficiaries of the faith and have the strongest interest in the Party's monopoly of political power. They serve the First Secretary of the Party and in turn they expect him to maintain their rights and privileges against encroachments by the state bureaucracy. There is a latent conflict between the two orders of officials, because the state bureaucrats (who in a Communist regime include all those who would be directors and managers of private economic enterprises in a capitalist society) commonly resent the interference of Party authorities in the specialized work they are doing, and may even take the view that the state could get on better if its political controllers were reduced to the role of mere ideological chaplains. When therefore the First Secretary of the Party becomes Prime Minister and is personally involved in the problems of state administration instead of simply running the Party as the 'directing nucleus' (the phrase used in the Soviet Constitution) of the system, he may gradually come to assume the point of view of the state rather than of the Party officialdom. The issue hardly arose during Stalin's regime because in his later years he ruled primarily through the secret police and was thus in a sense elevated in his personal despotism above both Party and state. But Khrushchev did not possess Stalin's secret police power; he rose to the top as the man of the Party apparatus and he continued to need its support. Nevertheless, as Prime Minister he became more and more absorbed in the problem of how to make the Soviet economy work, and his strongest purpose was to create an efficient economic administration. Finally he took the step of dividing the Party apparatus into agricultural and industrial sectors so that its members could be specialized for their tasks of administrative supervision. But this was to degrade the Party from its proper position as a unitary political organization above and distinct from the state. It was an intolerable affront to the *apparatchiki*, and it was only because he had become arrogant and careless after so many years of power that Khrushchev behaved as he did. The outcome was fatal to his political career. He had many enemies and he had committed serious blunders in both domestic and foreign policy, but he could weather all storms as long as he had the devoted support of the Party organization; when he lost it, he was finished. After his fall his 'reform' of the Party organization was immediately reversed.

After the political exit of Khrushchev the offices of First Secretary of the Party and Prime Minister of the government were again separated, being held respectively by Brezhnev and Kosygin. Thus after the successive attempts of Stalin and Khrushchev to combine the supreme powers of Party and state the Soviet political system reverted to the situation which had existed after the death of Lenin when Stalin was Secretary-General of the Party and Rykov Chairman of the Council of People's Commissars. This separation of powers not only provided the best safeguard against the exercise of an autocratic personal authority; it also best conserved the peculiar character of the Communist Party-state as a regime in which the normal organs of civil and military administration were to be permanently controlled by the Communist Party. In Marxist–Leninist theory the Party is an elite with a historical mission to transform a capitalist into a socialist society – and to lead it on to the ideal higher stage in which the state will 'wither away'; it must at all costs preserve its doctrinal purity, its integrity and its superiority to merely pragmatic considerations.

But was the CPSU as Leninist in spirit and in action in 1967 as it had been in 1917? There has been one necessary and irreversible change: the difference of generations. In 1967 there were very few individuals alive in Russia who had been Party members in 1917; there were not many who could remember the Revolution as an episode of their childhood. The great majority of the population of the Soviet Union had been born since 1917 and the bulk of the holders of political office had been brought up under the Soviet regime. The veterans of the Revolution would in any case gradually have died off or become incapacitated from natural causes, but Stalin had greatly accelerated the process by his wholesale slaughter of the 'Old Bolsheviks'. The Communists of the second generation differed greatly from those of the first. They had never had any experience of the pre-Soviet era; they only knew what the Party propagandists said about it. Unlike the revolutionaries of Lenin's generation who had so often lived abroad either as students or in exile, very few of the second generation had ever been outside the borders of Soviet territory – except perhaps as soldiers of an invading army. They had not struggled for the Communist cause as a goal that seemed remote and unrewarding until it was suddenly attained; they had found the Soviet regime ready-made and took it for granted. It was the society in which they grew up, the established order of things with all the instruments of coercion to enforce its authority and all the media of communication to justify its pretensions. It was a society whose beliefs and values nobody was permitted to question openly, and it was a society which the privileged and successful found very good. It was a society in which membership of the Communist Party was the road, and nearly always the only road, to important and lucrative appointments; to show zeal for the Party line of the moment as expounded in *Pravda* was the way to attract the favourable notice of one's superiors. But what was the real quality of faith under such conditions? It could be assumed that a man who risked arrest and imprisonment in Tsarist Russia for his political activity had a genuine conviction of the beliefs he professed; the same could not be said of a man when profession of the same belief was the sole passport to good employment. In the Russia of 1967 everyone – and not only Party members – outwardly accepted Communism, but nobody could say how far a sincere and ardent faith in it extended. One thing, however, could be asserted with confidence: that whether or not the *apparatchiki* of the Communist Party genuinely believed in their doctrine they had a vested interest in its maintenance and propagation. For them at least there was no other livelihood.

16.   Peaceful Coexistence

The Second World War was fought out until the surrender of Germany with what were later to become known as 'conventional' weapons – artillery, tanks, machine-guns, hand-grenades and bomber aircraft. War fought with these weapons could be immensely destructive, both of human life and of places of human habitation and production, but the destruction was still confined within certain limits; the armies fought each other on defined fronts, while the bomber fleets, though able to range far and wide over the territories of enemy countries, were able to accomplish only indecisive results as long as they carried only ordinary high explosive and incendiary bombs. The great bomber offensive against Germany fell short of the expectations of those who promoted it, and experience showed that civilian populations stood up to bombing more stoutly than had been anticipated. In the last stage of the war, when the Luftwaffe could no longer carry out heavy bombing attacks, 'flying bombs' and rockets were used by the Germans against England, but their warheads still contained nothing but old-fashioned explosives and the damage they could accomplish hardly justified the cost of their production. But at the end of the war against Japan, and accelerating that end, an entirely new type of bomb was used, and its advent marked the beginning of a new era in strategy and thus indirectly in the relations between sovereign states. The development of the new weaponry affected above all the conflict between Russia and the US which emerged after the end of the Second World War and the calculations on both sides of the risks of full military hostilities which might arise from it. Moreover, since the prospects of world Communism were at stake in this conflict, the ideology of Communism was also involved and had to be adjusted to an unprecedented situation.

Stalin, as we have seen, showed great caution as the conflict with the West grew sharper, and refrained from taking action which would have precipitated war during the blockade of West Berlin. He preferred to accept failure in his bid to obtain control of the city rather than face the dangers of a war against a coalition of the Western powers so soon after the conclusion of the war against Nazi Germany. But there was as yet no general theory of a need to avoid war as being inevitably self-destructive on account of the nature of the weapons available to the belligerents. As long as Stalin lived, the official military theory of the Soviet Union played down the importance of nuclear weapons, representing them as merely auxiliary to conventional forces and incapable of deciding the issue of a war by themselves. This may have been partly a tactic to keep up the morale of the Soviet forces during the period before the Soviet Union had produced its own atomic armoury, but it was not altogether untenable doctrine before the hydrogen bomb was added to the atomic stockpile, which was not until 1954, that is to say, after Stalin's death. With the production of the hydrogen bomb, however, and with the simultaneous development of long-range ballistic missiles, it became clear that it was possible for two powers with large nuclear armouries to inflict on each other an intolerable devastation by mutual bombardment with weapons against which there could be no adequate defence. The only way in which a nuclear power A could hope to overcome a comparable nuclear power B without being itself annihilated would be by a 'pre-emptive' surprise attack which would destroy B's bombers and missiles on the ground before they could be used; this was possible during the period before the 'hardening' of missile sites and the planting of missiles in submarines decisively reduced the vulnerability of the nuclear armouries to operations of the Pearl Harbor type. But the mere possibility enhanced the danger of war, for a power fearing a pre-emptive attack might decide at a time of acute international tension to do the pre-empting itself; war could thus come about through panic without either side deliberately intending it. The only safeguard was a reduction of international tension to a point below the danger level, and this was what Stalin's successors in the government of the Soviet Union proceeded to try to do. A new and more conciliatory attitude was manifest in Moscow soon after Stalin's death, and at the Geneva Conference of 1954, which brought about a temporary settlement in Indochina, diplomacy functioned more normally than it had done since the Big Three had met at Potsdam in the summer of 1945. There was a general sense of relaxation, of 'thaw' and of hope for the future, with a corresponding impression that the danger of war was now receding. This cooling-down in itself made war less likely.

It remained, however, for Communist leaders to recognize the implications of the new policy and to justify it theoretically in Marxist-Leninist terms. Hitherto Communists, following Lenin, had justified revolutionary war on principle and had held war with imperialist states to be sooner or later inevitable, though it would rest with the leadership in any particular case to decide whether or not to take risks of war in its foreign policy. The invasion of Russia by the Germans in 1941 in spite of Stalin's deal with Hitler had seemed to prove that war could not be avoided in a capitalist world, and the victorious outcome of that war had appeared to show that Communism was invincible and need not fear an encounter with even the most powerful foe. But how was such a view of world affairs to be reconciled with the new need to avoid war if possible for as far ahead as could be foreseen? If the official doctrine remained as it was, it would be open to critics within the Party – and such criticism was again possible now that Stalin was dead – to denounce the leadership for weakness and cowardice if it invoked the risk of war as justification for not taking a provocatively tough line in an international crisis. It was not enough therefore to work for some degree of *détente* in the actual conduct of foreign policy; under a regime in which all policies had to be based somehow on an ideology, a modification of theory was also necessary. This was done in two ways. In the first place, it was formally proclaimed at the Twentieth Congress of the CPSU in 1956 – the same at which the famous secret speech against Stalin was made by Khrushchev – that war was no longer 'fatally inevitable'; there was now a possibility of averting it altogether, in spite of the bellicosity of the imperialist warmongers, partly because the socialist camp headed by the Soviet Union had become strong enough to deter any attack and partly because popular movements for peace within the capitalist world had become sufficiently influential to restrain the warmongers through domestic politics. This formula was in accordance with the dogma that aggression could come only from the other side. But lest anyone should think that with the new strength of the socialist camp the time had come to further the ends of world revolution by bold and adventurous policies, it was explained in speeches by Soviet leaders that the nature of war in the new age was such that neither side would be able to escape utter devastation in an all-out nuclear war, so that traditional ideas of victory and defeat were no longer applicable.

The whole of Communist theory had to be adapted to the new conception of war as something that must be avoided except in self-defence. The doctrine had been one of revolutionary violence, and this violence, which naturally took the form of armed insurrection and civil war within individual states, could also take the form of war between states when 'states with different social systems' confronted one another in the international arena. The worldwide proletarian revolution, which was historically inevitable, could perhaps be brought about by a series of completely separate and self-sufficient revolutions in particular countries, but states in which the proletariat had been victorious, that is countries under Communist rule, had a duty to aid revolutions in countries still under the rule of capitalism, and the procedure by which the Soviet Union had helped to put Communist parties in power in a number of adjacent countries after the end of the Second World War appeared to provide a model for an indefinitely extending Communist conquest of the world. The United States had indeed rallied the capitalist world for the time being with its NATO alliance and its troops in Europe, but this need be no more than a temporary check; when conditions were favourable, the forces of Communism should press on, and if the Western powers should be so foolish as to treat a Soviet intervention as a *casus belli*, they would merely suffer the fate of Hitler's Germany and the final triumph of Communism would be accelerated. This was the natural way of thinking for a Russian Communist who had been brought up on the teachings of Lenin and had seen the Red Army marching into Vienna, Prague and Berlin. But now, if a full-scale international war had become too dangerous to be contemplated, such hopes and ambitions had to be renounced for the foreseeable future. How in this situation was a devout Marxist–Leninist to keep his faith in the predestined universal victory of the revolution?

The answer provided by Khrushchev was that the revolution was indeed destined to prevail, but by 'victory in peaceful competition with capitalism'. War must be ruled out and replaced by 'peaceful coexistence between states with different social systems', but the political struggle between them would continue and would be decided by economic means. The Soviet Union and the other Communist-ruled countries would simply outproduce the capitalist nations, developing the inherently superior capacity of a socialized economy to expand production and raise standards of living. When after a few years the masses throughout the world saw that the prosperity of the Soviet Union far exceeded that of the United States, they would be irresistibly attracted towards Communism and their governments would be unable to refuse their demands for imitation of the Soviet model. Thus, without any international war, and perhaps even without much in the way of violent revolutions, the whole world would be converted to Communism.

The idea that the Soviet Union would shortly succeed in surpassing the United States in *per capita* economic production and standards of living was superficially plausible in Russia in the mid 1950s when the momentum of post-war economic growth was still strong and the exhilaration of the victory over Germany still inspired a glowing optimism and self-confidence. As the years passed, however, the date for surpassing the U S economy receded further into the distance, and the victory over capitalism through peaceful competition looked as if it would have to be postponed for a long time.

Fortunately for the believing Communist the Khrushchev slogans did not entirely exclude methods which were more in keeping with the old ways. If the existence of the 'nuclear stalemate' or 'balance of terror' made it dangerous for the Soviet Union to challenge the U S to a mortal combat, there was still a fairly wide zone of the world in which violent actions could be promoted in the reasonable expectation that they would not lead to a nuclear exchange. Khrushchev developed the doctrine that the peaceful coexistence he so tirelessly advocated was not incompatible with moral and material support for 'wars of national liberation' – a category which covered activities as diverse as the Algerian revolt against France, Arab plans for the destruction of Israel, the armed infiltration from North into South Vietnam, Sukarno's confrontation against Malaysia, the Simba insurrection in the Congo and Castro's hate campaign against the United States. These movements might or might not be Communist-led; the important thing was that they were directed against the US or against her allies or protégés. By giving them political support, by sending them supplies of arms and by intervening diplomatically on their behalf – as when the Soviet Union used the veto to prevent any condemnation of the Indonesian attacks on Malaysia by the Security Council of the United Nations – Moscow carried on a dual policy, combining peaceful coexistence and the quest for a *détente* with promotion of local wars and revolutionary upheaval in various parts of the world. In these policies there was no consistent guiding principle beyond the calculation how far the policy in question would provoke the US. The Soviet Union was able to get away with a great deal of mischief-making because of the strength of the US desire for a *détente* – a desire which drew President Eisenhower into his ill-fated negotiations with Khrushchev over Berlin and continued to sway the State Department and US public opinion in spite of a series of rebuffs and disappointments. Once indeed the Russians went too far; by putting ballistic missiles into Cuba Khrushchev got a US reaction stronger and swifter than he had expected and he had to retreat with as much dignity as he could muster. But in Vietnam the boot was on the other foot; Vietnam was on the other side of the Pacific instead of being a close neighbour of the US in the western hemisphere and the American commitment to defend South Vietnam was half-hearted in comparison with the determination not to tolerate a Soviet nuclear base in the Caribbean. Massive supplies of arms, munitions and petrol were sent from the Soviet Union to North Vietnam to sustain the North Vietnamese effort to overrun the South, but fear of escalation was sufficient to deter the US from a naval blockade of Haiphong. A fantastic situation arose in which US troops were daily being killed by weapons sent from Russia for the purpose and the North Vietnamese enemy would not be able to wage war at all without these supplies, yet almost complete silence on the matter was maintained by the US press and in political speeches so as not to aggravate relations with Moscow. The Soviet Union was thus successful not merely in pinning down half a million US troops in South-East Asia and bleeding them by proxy without the loss of a single Russian soldier, but also in achieving this without even having to suffer any verbal unpleasantness from the victim of the operation.

In Indonesia and Egypt Soviet political enterprises were less successful. To Indonesia, led by the anti-imperialist Sukarno with his 'guided democracy' and his 'new emerging forces', Russia supplied large quantities of arms for use first against the Dutch in New Guinea and then against the British in Borneo and Malaya. The Dutch were evicted, but against the British petty raiding was not enough, and 'confrontation' ran down into a futile attrition while the economy, bedevilled by Sukarno's crazy economic policies, moved ever closer to total collapse; then a bungled Communist *coup* caused the Indonesian army to put to death nearly all the leaders of the Communist party – the largest in the world outside Communist-governed countries – and set up a dictatorship of the Right with the arms provided by Russia. In Egypt there was no such defection, but the arms lavishly provided by Moscow were lost in another way; when it came to the showdown with Israel, nearly all the bombers were destroyed on the ground and most of the tanks were wrecked or captured by the Israeli army. Russia was then called on to replace the equipment which had been lost, and did so rather than forfeit the influence gained by support for the Arab purpose of destroying Israel – an aspiration which had nothing to do with Communism or with the wrongs of the proletariat, but which was consonant with the interests of the Soviet Union because it set up an auction in which the United States and Britain could never bid high enough.

The political struggle of the Soviet Union with the

United States had indeed never ceased in spite of the slogan of peaceful coexistence, which in fact meant only that a head-on collision between the two superpowers became less likely after the hydrogen bomb was included in their armouries. In the historical perspective of international relations it can be said that once overwhelming preponderant power in the world was concentrated in two states, a rivalry between them for influence over other states was inevitable even if they had not become the representatives of two rival ideologies. But the ideological conflict not merely aggravated and embittered their antagonism, it meant that they were constantly drawn to take sides in violent domestic struggles taking place in other countries all over the world. Both sides as part of their rivalry were ready even to make alliances with states which did not share their own ideology; thus democratic America aligned itself with Franco's Spain and Ngo Dinh Diem's Vietnam in the cause of anti-Communism, and Communist Russia became the patron of Nasser's Egypt (which suppressed its local Communists) under the banner of anti-imperialism. But in all these disguises and transformations it remained the 'cold war' between two opposed systems of human society, and the only peace in their coexistence was that induced by an overriding mutual fear.

17. Polycentrism

At the time of his death Stalin was the acknowledged leader of the entire world Communist movement with the single exception of the Yugoslav Party. It was often said that Stalin was the Pope of all the Communists and that Moscow was their Rome. Certainly the international movement presented an impressively united front to the rest of the world. This had, however, the disadvantage that hostile propaganda could represent Communism as a single worldwide conspiracy centred in the Kremlin and argue persuasively that as all Communists were thus under Russian control, any Communist-led revolution anywhere must be instigated from Moscow and extend the power of the Soviet Union if successful.

The Yugoslav exception remained an exception for a long time, for no other Communist party officially sided with Yugoslavia although there were widespread secret sympathies for Tito's stand. The quarrel arose from Tito's determination to be master in his own house, but the condition of his ability to defy Stalin without destroying the Communist regime in Yugoslavia was the position of national leadership he had attained through his command of the 'Partisan' guerrilla forces of resistance to the German army of occupation during the war. The Communist parties ruling in other East and Central European countries had too little basis of support among the peoples they governed and were too dependent on Soviet support to think, at any rate during the early post-war years and while Stalin was alive, of asserting their independence from Moscow. Moreover, Stalin had his own methods for enforcing discipline, even without direct use of the military forces which still remained not only in East Germany, but also in Poland, Rumania and Hungary. In each party there were rivals of the existing leaders who were in contact with the Soviet intelligence services and were available for bringing about a change in the leadership if it were to prove unsatisfactory from a Soviet point of view. The knowledge that they could at any time be thus replaced was a potent factor in keeping the leaders of Communist parties in the satellite countries in line with Soviet policies. Tito, however, objected to this kind of supervision. He was aware that his Party had been deeply infiltrated by the Soviet intelligence service and that there was in it a clique which was ready to take over power from him if he were too unruly. He moved to rid himself of the Russian agents and advisers who surrounded him, and the measures he took provoked Soviet reprimands for unfriendly action; when Tito refused to be intimidated, tension increased and led finally to a rupture of relations between the two Parties. The Soviet Union then took steps to move the whole Communist international movement against the rebellious Yugoslavs, and the other parties duly rallied to the Soviet side in the dispute. Tito was denounced as a Fascist and an agent of imperialism. Passing from words to action, the Soviet *bloc* countries applied economic sanctions by cutting off their trade with Yugoslavia, but the Yugoslavs obtained commercial credits from the United States, and although this was naturally taken by their enemies as proof that the whole affair had been engineered in Wall Street, Tito was thus able to hold out. His stand received strong support from the Yugoslav people; even in quarters adverse to Communism the defiance of a Great Power whose overbearing behaviour had alienated national sentiment now produced strong patriotic emotions in Tito's favour. It was clear that nothing but a military invasion could break Tito's recalcitrance, and, as we have seen,[1] Stalin shrank from this last resort. As a result of the quarrel

1. See p. 160.

Yugoslavia remained estranged from all other Communist-ruled states as long as Stalin was alive, but it remained itself Communist and the measure of economic support it received from the West did not involve it in any return to capitalism. In Belgrade it was said, with characteristic Yugoslav modesty, that 'the world is now divided into three parts: East, West and Yugoslavia'.

For Stalin the insubordination of Tito was an affront, but he could put up with it as long as the infection did not spread, and it did not spread to any significant extent. There were a number of purge trials in the satellite states in which the victims were accused among other things of being in league with Tito, but some at least of these accusations were false, and the real sympathy for the Yugoslav cause was nowhere sufficient to capture or overturn the leadership of a party.

All the East European states which came under Communist rule in 1945 and the years following were, with the exception of Germany, relatively small in comparison with the Soviet Union and were therefore liable to fall under the influence of a neighbouring Great Power. Germany had been a Great Power and was still the second nation of Europe in respect of population, but the Germans had been totally defeated and disarmed and had to carry the burden of guilt for Hitler's war; moreover, the East German government was the most unpopular of all the satellite regimes and the most dependent on Soviet backing, so that Stalin could count on his Ulbricht more than on anyone else to be evermore a puppet. In the opposite direction from Moscow, however, in the east of Asia there was a new Communist regime which commanded the most numerous nation of the world, one which had been not among the defeated but among the victorious nations of the Second World War and one which in the past had regarded itself as the only real source of human civilization. It was inherently unlikely that this nation would be willing for long to play a secondary role in the international Communist movement. The leader of the Chinese Communists, Mao Tse-tung – he had been their leader since 1935 – had already shown a marked spirit of independence in the days when he was still fighting against the government of Chiang Kai-shek, and he could be expected to be even less willing to do what he was told when he was installed in power in Peking as a ruler of more than 500 million people. That there was no quarrel between Stalin and Mao comparable to the rift between Stalin and Tito must be ascribed to factors operative on both sides during Stalin's lifetime. On his side there was the experience of the Tito affair; by the time Mao had beaten the armies of the Kuomintang and set up the Chinese People's Republic, Stalin had had time to reflect on the lessons of his setback in Yugoslavia and the unwisdom of trying to ride a proud people with too tight a rein when there was no means of coercing them without open war. He no doubt appreciated the fact that China was a bigger country than Yugoslavia and realized that if he found it imprudent to invade Yugoslavia he would be even less prepared to undertake the military conquest of China. He therefore treated Mao Tse-tung with great consideration and deference; Mao visited the Soviet Union soon after proclamation of the Chinese People's Republic and does not appear to have had any cause for complaint over his reception. A military alliance was concluded which could be invoked in the event of a US attack on Communist China. Then came the Korean war and the Chinese intervention against the United Nations forces. The Soviet Union played its part both by supplying arms to China and by a diplomatic stand which deterred the United States and its allies from direct action against Chinese territory for fear of bringing about a general war. Up to the time of Stalin's death, therefore, Sino–Soviet relations remained harmonious with no sign of the rending discords that were to come later.

After Stalin had breathed his last, it was at once obvious that there could be no successor who would enjoy the personal authority he had possessed. His empire, if it could be held together at all, would have to be directed more by persuasion and less by words of command than it had been under the great *Vozhd*.[2] Khrushchev, who as First Party Secretary now handled relations of the C.P.S.U with other Communist parties, was certainly aware of this and set out to be as flexible and conciliatory as he could in dealing with foreign comrades. Unfortunately his very suppleness soon got him into trouble. He conceived the idea of calling off the outlawry of Tito and imagined that he could win great credit for himself by bringing him back into the Communist fold. Without adequate political preparation he went to Belgrade in 1955 to tell Tito that all was forgiven and that Stalin's ban on him was lifted. Tito, however, was not asking to be forgiven; he considered himself the aggrieved party, and while graciously accepting what he chose to regard as an apology from the CPSU for the way he had been treated, he declined to modify in any way the heretical deviation from Marxist–Leninist doctrine in which the Yugoslavs had indulged since their break with Russia. Khrushchev's visit to Belgrade thus turned out to be a journey to Canossa rather than a triumphant missionary enterprise. It was in effect an exculpation of heresy and a licence to other parties to follow the Titoist road. It annoyed and demoralized those leaders who had been most faithful to Moscow during the dispute with Tito, for it was indeed a case of the Parable of the Prodigal Son, with the difference that the prodigal for whom the fatted calf was metaphorically killed by Khrushchev had not provided even the self-interested expression of repentance uttered by his prototype in the Biblical story.

The adverse effects of Khrushchev's blundering reconciliation with Tito were of small account, however, in comparison with those produced by the secret speech against Stalin at the Twentieth Congress of the CPSU

2. A Russian word habitually applied to Stalin and having something of the same force as *Führer* in Nazi German usage.

and its subsequent publication. The prestige of Communism, or at least of Soviet leadership, underwent a disastrous slump in the eyes not only of ordinary citizens of the 'people's democracies', but also of the Communists themselves, who were covered with confusion at the sudden debunking in Moscow of the glorious captain under whose banner they had obtained power. In October of 1956 the discontent and disillusionment flared up in movements of national revolt in Poland and Hungary.

In order to understand what followed it must be borne in mind that there were great differences among the Communist states of Europe in their relations to Russia apart from the issue of inter-party relations. Poland and Czechoslovakia were bound to Russia in the post-war period, not merely by the fact that they had Communist governments, but even more by their need of Russian protection against a possible German *revanche*. Poland had annexed all German territory up to the Oder–Neisse line and expelled its German inhabitants; Czechoslovakia had driven out its three million Sudeten Germans whose existence within the frontiers of the Czech state as drawn in 1919 had provided Hitler with his pretext for aggression. Neither Poland nor Czechoslovakia could have any security in a world in which Germany might again become powerful unless they could rely on the backing of the Soviet Union. There was a difference between the Poles and the Czechs in their historical and traditional experience and traditional sentiments as regards Russia; the Poles were as hostile to Russia as the Czechs were friendly in their national feelings. But both countries – or at any rate their most politically conscious citizens, whether Communist or anti-Communist – were aware that they could not go against Russia with a vengeful Germany in their rear.

A somewhat similar situation prevailed in Bulgaria, a country which was not only Slav but had been liberated from the rule of the Turks by a Russian army. For the Bulgarians since 1913 the main national enemy had been

Greece, which by the peace settlements of 1913 and 1919 had obtained not only Salonika and Kavalla, but the whole seaboard of the Aegean eastward to the Maritza. In order to gain or regain these territories (and those of Serbian or Yugoslav Macedonia) Bulgaria had allied herself with Germany in both World Wars. But after the Russians had entered Bulgaria in 1944 and put the Bulgarian Communists in power in Sofia they revived in favour of a pro-Russian regime the Bulgarian claim to the Aegean littoral. In the making of the peace treaties with the Axis satellites Britain and the United States protested that they had never heard of a defeated nation claiming territory from a victorious one, and Bulgaria did not get any part of Greece, but Russia had established herself as a champion of Bulgarian national aspirations, and this situation became more or less permanent, with the result that Bulgaria, like Poland and Czechoslovakia, became a country looking to Moscow for help in the fundamentals of its foreign policy.

Quite different was the position of Hungary and Rumania in relation to Russia. These countries had no common frontiers with Germany and did not share the fears of a German *revanche* which obsessed the Poles and Czechs. Nor did they, like Bulgaria, cherish national aspirations which they expected the Russians one day to enable them to fulfil. They had bitter memories of the Russian invasions of 1944 without any compensating hopes of future Russian protection or backing. Apart from the few hard-core Communists they regarded themselves as defeated and humiliated nations who might some time get a chance to throw off the Russian yoke. This background explains both the violent and heroic, but ineffectual, Hungarian rising of 1956, and the more subtle and successful anti-Russian policy pursued by Rumania since 1962.

The Polish move for independence in the autumn of 1956 was Titoist in that it was a defiance of Russia under the leadership of the national Communist party. It produced great tension culminating in the dramatic confrontation when Khrushchev appeared at a meeting of the Polish Communist Central Committee in the company of several Russian generals in a vain attempt to bully the Polish Party into submission. In the end a compromise agreement was reached without the firing of guns. In Hungary, on the other hand, the national uprising was both anti-Russian and anti-Communist; Communist rule was definitely brought to an end and a multi-party democracy was proclaimed. The Soviet Union intervened with strong military forces and restored Communist rule, though under a leadership less harsh than that which had preceded the rising. By using force to crush the revolt, the Soviet Union gave notice that any similar attempt in future to overthrow an established Communist regime would likewise meet with Russian military intervention.

Rumania did not make any move in 1956 and was duly intimidated by the brutal repression in Budapest. But a few years later the split in the international Communist movement between the Soviet Union and the Chinese People's Republic provided an opportunity for the Rumanian party leadership to manoeuvre between the two sides and attain a position of greatly increased independence. The quarrel between Moscow and Peking is dealt with in the next chapter of this book; it is sufficient to point out that its effect in Europe was to put the non-Soviet parties in a stronger position than before because Moscow now needed their support in the struggle against Maoism and could not afford to antagonize them. The Rumanian leaders exploited this situation in order to resist Russian pressures for economic arrangements under which Rumania would concentrate on primary products and get its industrial goods from Russia. The Rumanians said this involved treating Rumania as a colonial country and the controversy aroused all the nationalist emotions of the Rumanian people which were for the first time arrayed behind their Communist government. Rumania's challenge to Russian ascendancy was more serious than Yugoslavia's had been because Rumania was adjacent to the frontiers of the Soviet Union, as Yugoslavia was not, but Moscow was reluctant to use force and the Rumanian leaders stopped just short of provoking it.

It was in Western Europe, however, that the new doctrine of 'polycentrism', of the fundamental autonomy of national Communist parties, was officially formulated. It made its appearance soon after the denunciation of Stalin at the Twentieth Congress of the CPSU. The Communists of Western Europe recognized by 1956 that they had very little prospect of making successful violent revolutions on the classic Bolshevik model, but good opportunities of playing a political role in their respective countries if they could improve their image in the eyes of their peoples and dissociate themselves from the 'asiatic' features of Communist rule in Russia. They recalled that Marx and Engels had been men of the West, not Russians, and that the socialist cause had flourished in Western Europe before it had won adherents on the Neva. Togliatti, who had been closer to Stalin than any other non-Soviet Communist except Gottwald, successfully pretended that he had never known what was going on in Russia and made himself the spokesman for a more humane and 'liberal' Communism which would go its own way and devise its own tactics in the conditions of advanced industrial and politically democratic societies without regard to directives from the Kremlin. But the new polycentrists of Western Europe were still on the side of the Russo–Marxists of Moscow against the still more alien Sino–Marxists of Peking.

18. Maoism

The variant of Communism known as Maoism has from its inception had a double character; it has been in part a genuine ideological opposition to the form of Communism which has prevailed in the Soviet Union since the death of Stalin, but it has also in part arisen from a clash of national interests and of even more fundamental ethnic attitudes between Russia and China. The ideological disapproval of Russian 'revisionism' would probably have grown in Peking with the development of Soviet policies under Khrushchev even if there had been no Soviet actions which seemed to the Chinese to disregard their national interests and imply a will to relegate them permanently to an inferior status. But since there *were* such actions the bitterness of a national enmity was added to the animosity of an ideological conflict. The Maoists themselves would not indeed distinguish between the two aspects; they would say that Soviet actions at the expense of Chinese national interests were simply an inevitable consequence of the corruption of the CPSU by a revisionist ideology. But behind the doctrinal controversies there were on both sides factors of national pride with overtones of chauvinist arrogance which set the two regimes on a collision course in spite of their common profession of the Marxist–Leninist faith

For an understanding of the ideological divergence between Peking and Moscow the chronology is of fundamental importance. As has already been pointed out,[1] post-Stalin Russia was dominated by Communists of the second generation, who were in many ways different from those of the first. Chinese Communism, on the other

1. See p. 169.

hand, a decade after the founding of the Chinese People's Republic, was still a first-generation movement led by men who had spent long years in the revolutionary underground or carrying on guerrilla warfare in the countryside. The Chinese People's Republic set up in 1949 was thirty-two years younger than the Soviet Union dating from 1917. It was only to be expected that the Chinese Communists in the period after Stalin's death should display the qualities of fanatical fervour, revolutionary enthusiasm and disdain for mere material well-being which had been characteristic of the Old Bolsheviks but were very far from being characteristic of their successors in the Russia of Khrushchev and Brezhnev. To the Chinese Communists their Russian comrades seemed to be lacking in zeal, to have lost the sense of revolutionary dedication and to have become *embourgeoisés*. To the Russians the Chinese appeared as excessively militant, callow and immature. The mutual disapproval involved in these attitudes might have remained a matter of sentiment, but from the time of the Twentieth Congress of the CPSU in 1956 it became possible for the Chinese to accuse the Russian Communists of an ideological back-sliding corresponding to, but much more serious than, the decline of their revolutionary *élan*. At that Congress the Soviet Party did indeed drastically modify accepted Marxist–Leninist doctrine, both by the claim that war was no longer inevitable in international relations and by the thesis that Communist parties might obtain power by non-violent means. In neither case did the CPSU adequately consult other parties in the international movement before introducing these innovations into Communist theory.

In their later contention that the trend manifest at the Twentieth Congress was one of 'revisionism' – a term of abuse in Marxist circles ever since it had been applied to Bernstein and his school in the 1890s – the Chinese undoubtedly had the better of the theoretical argument. The decisions of the Twentieth Congress were a repudiation of Lenin and of the Marx of the *Communist Manifesto*. On the other hand the later Marx and his followers, the orthodox Social Democrats of Germany and the Russian Mensheviks, who rejected the overt revisionism of Bernstein, had created precedents for the doctrinal innovations of the Twentieth Congress by toning down the original Marxist emphasis on armed violence as the essential means of revolution. But Lenin had stood for a reversion to the *Communist Manifesto*, and acceptance of the need for the use of force had been a condition for the admission of any party as a member of the Comintern. Marxism–Leninism meant, therefore, not simply that the doctrine of Lenin had been added on to that of Marx, but that Marxism itself was to be interpreted in a Leninist way. In reasserting the primacy of violence as a means of revolution the Chinese Communists certainly stood closer than Khrushchev did to the *Communist Manifesto* and to the teaching of Lenin. The Soviet Communists, however, implicitly if not explicitly, claimed the right to modify Marxist–Leninist doctrine on their own authority as the sole legitimate heirs of Marx and Lenin. This claim was challenged by the Chinese, as it had already been challenged by the Yugoslavs, with the difference that, whereas the Yugoslav deviation was to the right of the line laid down by the CPSU – in the direction of European liberalism – the Chinese deviation was to the left of it – in the direction of greater revolutionary militancy and extremism.

The Chinese Communists did not immediately play their ideological cards against Moscow because they still had hopes of a lavish economic and military aid from the Soviet Union which would enable them to advance rapidly to the Great Power position to which they aspired. At the gathering of Communist parties in Moscow in November 1957 to celebrate the fortieth anniversary of the Bolshevik Revolution Mao Tse-tung not only refrained from attacking the decisions of the Twentieth Congress, but urged that the declaration to be put out in the name of the governing Communist parties should describe the camp of the socialist countries as 'headed by the Soviet Union'. There can be no doubt, however, that, in Mao's mind, this leadership from Moscow was to be conditional on its being exerted in the right direction, that is to say in a strenuous contest with the enemy camp headed by the US; it was not a leadership which he was prepared to follow if it led to 'capitulation' to imperialism.

Chinese hopes of Soviet economic and military help and of victorious advances by the socialist camp under the strategic direction of 'the first and mightiest socialist Power' were, nevertheless, grievously disappointed in the years following the Moscow meeting of 1957. The economic aid was less than was expected. Much more serious was the Soviet refusal to help China to produce nuclear weapons. This raised a fundamental question of status. The Chinese suspected, and with good reason, that the Soviet Union did not wish China to advance too fast or to attain equality with Soviet power in the field of the most decisive modern arms. The Chinese sense of solidarity with Russia was deeply eroded by awareness that Moscow sought to hold back rather than to promote China's development, and disillusionment was transformed into bitter indignation when it was found that far from leading the socialist camp to battle with the imperialists Khrushchev was aiming at a bilateral diplomatic deal with the US, in which Chinese interests would be ignored. The Chinese Communist leaders watched with dismay the moves of Soviet policy in 1959 which led up to the Camp David meeting between Khrushchev and President Eisenhower. There is no evidence that Khrushchev made any attempt to promote the interests of China in his diplomatic quest; if he had been able, as he hoped, to get his way over Berlin, he would have been quite willing for China to be left out in the cold. Moreover, just before the Camp David negotiations the Soviet government perpetrated what was in Chinese eyes an unforgivable betrayal both of the spirit of the Russo–Chinese alliance and of international Communist solidarity by taking up a neutral position over the India–China border dispute (which led to an armed clash in the summer of 1959) instead of giving moral and political support to China. To be neutral in a conflict between a Communist and a bourgeois state was indeed something unheard-of; it had hitherto been regarded as axiomatic that in such a quarrel the bourgeois state must be the aggressor.

The Chinese exasperation at Khrushchev's behaviour resulted in the launching of an ideological campaign against revisionism in which the Soviet Union was plainly accused of heresy, though the language used was still restrained and not yet characterized by the vituperative excesses which were to mark later stages of the controversy. It was now Khrushchev's turn to become angry; he resolved to punish the Chinese for their impertinence and force them into submission by economic sanctions which he reckoned they would be unable to withstand. He abruptly withdrew from China all the Russian engineers and other technical experts who had been sent to assist in China's industrialization; some of them took away plans and blueprints essential for the construction of new plants and installations. But this crude attempt at coercion of China had an effect opposite to what Khrushchev had expected; instead of bringing the Chinese to their knees it provoked a most intense resentment, an accentuation of the nationalist and ethnocentric tendency in Chinese Communism, and a determination to 'go it alone' in spite of all difficulties.

A conference of nearly all the Communist parties of the world was held in Moscow in November and December 1960 in an attempt to resolve the differences between the Soviet and Chinese parties, but, although a joint declaration was in the end agreed on, it was so vague that fresh disputes soon broke out over its interpretation. Further efforts at reconciliation all broke down, and not even

Khrushchev's fall in October 1964 brought about an appeasement. It was clear that basic national attitudes had become involved, and that a Russian dislike and contempt for the Chinese was more than matched by the growth in China of a spirit of self-admiring arrogance which revived in a new form the traditional and almost instinctive concept of the Middle Kingdom as the sole source of civilization and wisdom in a world of barbarians. This trend coincided with the growth of a fervent personality cult of Mao Tse-tung inside China and an increase of self-assurance and intransigence in Mao himself. In the first phase of the so-called Sino–Soviet Dispute Mao was clearly reacting to the extremely tactless and provocative behaviour of Khrushchev, but later, from the end of 1964 onwards, the boot appeared to be on the other foot; the successors of Khrushchev were ready for a reasonable compromise, but Mao became more and more truculent.

Maoism now developed into a distinct ideology. Its central feature was a new theory of world revolution to be achieved, not by uprisings of the industrial proletariat in big cities, but by peasant guerrilla insurrections on the model of the one which under Mao's leadership had been so successful in China. The idea of peaceful coexistence between states with different social systems was rejected as a surrender to imperialism, and it was declared to be Communist China's historic mission to lead and assist the peoples of the colonial and semi-colonial regions of the world in Asia, Africa and Latin America in revolutionary wars of 'national liberation'. Russia could not give such leadership, not merely because the post-Stalin generation in the CPSU had been corrupted by revisionism, but also because in any case Russia's revolutionary experience had been that of making a revolution in an urban industrial environment; this might qualify the Russian Communists for giving advice and direction in other industrial societies, but not as guides for those parts of the world which remained overwhelmingly agrarian. Moreover, whatever Marx might have expected, it was now in this zone, in the underdeveloped pre-industrial regions of the globe, that there was the greatest discontent, instability and disorder, with correspondingly good prospects for the seizure of power by a well organized revolutionary force. It was difficult on a detached consideration of Marxist theory to say whether this idea set Maoism to the right or to the left of the Communist orthodoxy of Moscow. The Maoist emphasis on the revolutionary potential of the peasants and of backward agrarian peoples was fundamentally a right-wing deviation and in the days when the official leadership of the Chinese Communist Party had been leftist Mao had been regarded as belonging to a right-wing opposition.[2] On the other hand, in a period when the Soviet line favoured 'soft' tactics in response to the political situation it confronted in Europe and America, the hard militant extremism of the Maoists put them on the left of the world Communist movement, and that was the way they saw themselves, as was implied in their persistent denunciation of the Russian Communists as revisionists.

The strength of Maoism inside China lay in its appeal to nationalist patriotic sentiments. It was exciting and exhilarating for the Chinese, still suffering from the psychic wounds inflicted by the humiliations of the nineteenth century, to reject the tutelage of Russia as they had already rejected that of the West, to affirm a total independence and self-reliance, and to claim a worldwide leadership of progressive forces as the only true heirs of the Marxist–Leninist faith. Such emotions, however, were hardly sufficient to sustain China over the years unless there were to be substantial results to show for a policy which antagonized both Russia and the West simultaneously. Unfortunately the policy failed to yield successes commensurate with the strains and tensions which it involved. Among the other Communist states only

2. John M. Rue, *Mao Tse-tung in Opposition 1927–1935* (Stanford U.P., 1966).

Albania was unreservedly on the side of China in the conflict with Moscow; this strange alliance, which earned for the little Balkan country the satirical title of 'China's first European colony', was due primarily to the deep Albanian antipathy towards Yugoslavia, which made the Albanians anti-Russian when Russia and Yugoslavia were reconciled. In Asia North Korea and North Vietnam at first inclined towards the Chinese side, but were later drawn back towards the Soviet Union, partly by their dependence on Soviet economic and military aid – with which China was unable to compete – and partly because of the Maoist regime's excessive paternalism towards them. Mongolia, which had been formally a part of China's sovereign territory until 1945, adhered firmly to the Soviet side. Cuba, in spite of the affinity of the Maoist and Castroite conceptions of revolutionary warfare, had to toe the Soviet line in order to obtain essential supplies, and Castro picked a quarrel with Peking over rice and sugar in order to keep his record straight with Moscow. Outside the sector of Communist-ruled states the great majority of the Communist parties of the world were on the side of the Soviet Union, although a number of them were opposed to the idea of holding a world conference for the purpose of excommunicating China and thus formally acknowledging the split in the international movement. If Mao had hoped to wrest the international leadership away from Moscow, at any rate in countries outside Europe, the outcome must have been very disappointing to him. The lack of success with established Communist parties would not have mattered so much, however, if the Maoists had been able to make a successful revolution somewhere in the world, but they failed to do so. A vigorous activity in Africa over several years produced no result except to cause several African governments which had recognized the Chinese People's Republic to break off diplomatic relations with it; a promising insurrection in the Congo petered out with a massacre of white hostages in Stanleyville as its most memorable achievement. In South Vietnam the Communists, using guerrilla tactics originally learned from China and developed by them in their war against the French, came near to overthrowing the U S-supported South Vietnam government, but a massive U S military intervention kept them out of Saigon, and as the struggle became increasingly one between the U S and the regular military forces of North Vietnam, the latter became more and more dependent on the Soviet Union and East European Communist countries for military equipment and supplies which China was unable to provide, so that, even if North Vietnam were to be victorious, the triumph would no longer accrue exclusively, or even mainly, to Chinese help and inspiration. Peking, having accused the Soviet Union of collusion with U S imperialism in Vietnam, rejected Soviet proposals for co-operation in aid to Hanoi and even obstructed deliveries of Soviet war material to Vietnam across China. This attitude further marred the image of Mao's China with Communists abroad, for it was incompatible with the Chinese profession of a single-minded devotion to the anti-imperialist cause; Peking's behaviour appeared both spiteful and hypocritical.

In 1965 Chinese Communist foreign policy suffered two major disasters. In Indonesia a bungled Communist *coup d'état*, in which China was widely believed to have had a hand, led to a counter-revolution in which the Indonesian Communist Party, the largest in the world outside the countries under Communist rule and one of those most favourable to the Peking line, was ruthlessly suppressed. The embittered anti-Western policy of Sukarno was abandoned by the new holders of power, and the projected congress of N E F O ('the New Emerging Forces'), which was intended to be a rival to the United Nations and for which China was building a magnificent headquarters in Djakarta, was cancelled. Even worse was the setback for China from the outcome of the brief war between India and Pakistan. In pursuit of its quarrel with India the Chinese People's Republic had concluded an informal alliance with Pakistan, and during the fighting had made threatening gestures against India in order to tie down as many Indian troops as possible in the Himalayas. But Russia and the US combined to press a cease-fire on the combatants and afterwards they both accepted Soviet mediation for a settlement; the conference was held in Tashkent, which was chosen by the Soviet Union in order to emphasize its position as an Asian power and the total exclusion of China from any say in the proceedings.

In the domestic field the isolation of China seriously retarded the country's economic progress. In the mid 1960s China was the only underdeveloped country receiving virtually no economic aid either from the West or from the Soviet *bloc*. Industrial plans had fallen far short of what had been envisaged in the previous decade, and the deficiencies of Chinese agriculture compelled Peking to spend a large part of its scarce foreign exchange, so badly needed for buying capital goods, on purchases of grain in Canada and Australia.

In these circumstances it was inevitable that the more pragmatically minded among the Chinese Communist leaders should consider among themselves how their country might emerge from its unprofitable isolation. The difficulty was that Mao Tse-tung was deeply committed to the current policy and that his conviction of his own unique wisdom only increased with his advancing age. There could be no question of deposing him for he had led the Party since 1935 and had been the founder of the People's Republic. But it might be possible to deprive him of effective power while keeping him as a figurehead. As Chairman of the Party[3] he did not directly control the Party organization and he no longer held any State office. A combination of Teng Hsiao-ping, the Secretary-General of the Party, Liu Shao-chi, the

3. The post of Party Chairman was a Chinese speciality; it did not exist in the CPSU.

Chairman of the Republic (with extensive constitutional powers as Head of State), and Peng Chen, Mayor of Peking and First Secretary of the Party in the capital, was strong enough to take the supreme direction of affairs out of Mao's hands, and they appear in effect to have done so when Mao became aware that he was losing control of the Party and launched a political counter-offensive. This was carried out under the cover of the so-called Great Proletarian Cultural Revolution, which had not begun as a power struggle between rival leaders, but as a campaign – not the first, but more thorough and far-reaching than any which had preceded it – to root out insufficiently revolutionary elements from the professions of literature, journalism and education. The campaign could easily be transformed into a purge of the Party because some of the writers attacked had enjoyed the patronage of high Party personalities. As the Cultural Revolution developed, it was pointed against 'a handful of persons in authority who have taken the capitalist road'; Peng Chen was driven from office, and then it was the turn of Teng and Liu. The outstanding feature of the Cultural Revolution was the support of the Army, which Mao skilfully played off against the Party. But the Army by itself was still not enough, and the late summer of 1966 saw the emergence of the Red Guards, a militia recruited from students and schoolchildren dedicated to a fanatical cult of Mao and his 'Thought' as embodied in a little book of quotations from his works printed and distributed by the Army in millions of copies. This mobilization of the young initially enabled Mao to dislodge many of his opponents from their positions in Party and State, but the movement thus promoted had in it highly dangerous trends towards hooliganism and anarchy, and it was not easy to co-ordinate its actions with those of the Army. Stalin in a somewhat similar situation in 1934 to 1938 had dealt with the opposition to his autocracy by means of the secret police, and he had been able to carry out his proscription without either wrecking the Communist Party or producing a civil war. Mao on the other hand lost control of his own purge; military commanders began to take independent initiatives to meet breakdowns of the state administration, and fighting between Maoist and anti-Maoist forces brought chaos to large areas of the country. Meanwhile, mob outrages by Red Guards against foreign diplomats and embassies in disregard of all accepted usages of international relations merely intensified Communist China's international isolation, and even countries which had been most friendly to China, such as Burma, Nepal and Cambodia, were alienated by the openly subversive behaviour of Maoists in the local Chinese communities. Mao's victory, such as it was, appeared to have been gained only at the cost of a further deterioration in the position of the Chinese Communist regime, both in domestic and in foreign affairs.

19. Communism and the Third World

With the formation of the N A T O and Warsaw Pact *blocs* of states bound together by treaties of alliance most of the nations of Europe were aligned on one side or the other of a line which was drawn on a basis of ideology but was also a demarcation between the spheres of influence of the two most powerful nations in the world. In Asia the Soviet Union had an alliance with the Chinese People's Republic (which was a political reality until a late stage of the Sino–Soviet Dispute) and several countries were linked with the U S and Britain in the Baghdad (later C E N T O) and S E A T O combinations, while Japan was aligned with the U S under a Security Pact. But many Asian countries, and notably India, were unwilling to join either side and made a principle of 'neutralism' or 'non-alignment' in the conflict between the Western and Soviet *blocs*. The newly independent states of Africa, geographically remote from the zones of conflict between Russia and the West, all followed the same line and tended to look to India as their model and leader in the international field. Thus the non-aligned countries of Asia and Africa came to form a group, not bound together by treaties of alliance, but loosely united by a common attitude towards the two great power *blocs*. In consequence this group came to be known as 'the Third World'.

All these countries were in 1945 by Marxist classification either colonial or semi-colonial. The colonial countries were those actually under the administrative control of European powers, whether as territories under their full sovereignty or as protectorates; the semi-colonial were countries formally independent, but economically so weak that they were dependent on foreign loans and foreign capital investments for their national economic existence. All these countries were 'backward' or 'under-developed' in comparison with the industrially evolved nations; some of them were rich in primary products, such as petroleum, copper, tin, cotton, rubber or rice, but none of them was industrially advanced. Viewed from an economic point of view, all were in much the same position in relation to Western capitalism, whether they were colonially governed or not, and in Marxist theory any capitalist country which had dominant economic influence over an underdeveloped one was 'imperialist' whether it had a colonial administration or not. It was because of this way of classifying countries that the Communists after 1945 could represent the US as imperialist – indeed as the imperialist nation *par excellence* – in spite of the fact that after conceding independence to the Philippines it had no longer any formal colonial control outside its own borders.[1] The people of the US, who identified imperialism with colonialism, could not understand how they could be charged with imperialism; they had the most lively sympathy for peoples striving to gain independence from European colonial rule – as for the Indonesians against the Dutch or the Algerians against the French – and it was very galling for them to be told later on by a Sukarno or a Boumedienne that they were the worst imperialists in the world. As the European colonial powers relinquished one by one their colonies and protectorates in Asia and Africa, they graduated from the category of colonialists to that of imperialists, but a special category of 'neo-colonialists' was devised for ex-colonial powers which still retained large economic interests in their former colonies.

The principle of neutralism now asserted by most of

1. Puerto Rico was still an exception, but it was on such a small scale that it did not invalidate the general proposition that the USA after 1945 was not a colonial power in the traditional sense.

the Third World countries was a new one in as much as neutrality in international relations had previously been a concept applicable only to war, in which it was a legally defined status with certain rights and obligations. The meaning of the term was now extended to cover mere non-participation in peacetime systems of military alliances; it did not and could not imply an absolute impartiality between the two main camps in world affairs, for in that sense a perfect neutrality was not within the range of practical politics. In fact the Third World inevitably became a field for political rivalry between the Communist powers and the West. The Western capitalist countries had the greater capacity to provide the economic aid so badly needed by the underdeveloped countries; on the other hand, the general political momentum of the Third World countries was internally towards the Left and externally towards conflict with the former colonial powers – especially where there had been a prolonged and embittered struggle for independence – or nations with large capital investments in local enterprises. Thus the Communist powers were able to obtain influence and exert political pressures on the governments of these countries greatly in excess of their capacity to bid in terms of economic aid. Generally speaking, organized Communist parties were weak in the Third World countries, India and Indonesia being the outstanding exceptions, and in many African countries they were virtually non-existent, but the intelligentsia and students were everywhere attracted by the Soviet or Chinese economic models, not so much as examples of successful revolution against industrial capitalism – which would hardly be relevant where modern industry was still in its infancy – but as patterns of rapid modernization and economic self-development without dependence on a foreign capital market.

Fear of Soviet or Chinese military aggression was not a factor in the Afro-Asian countries except in a few which were closely adjacent to Soviet or Chinese power.

Turkey and Persia, with long experience of past Russian encroachments, were ready to accept the protection of NATO or CENTO alliances, and in the Far East Siam and South Vietnam, feeling themselves threatened by the Chinese-supported Communist power in North Vietnam, looked to America. The motives of Pakistan for entering the CENTO and SEATO alliances were less simple; since the external tensions of Pakistan were neither with the Soviet Union nor with Communist China, but with India, it may be presumed that at least part of the Pakistan government's purpose in joining these essentially anti-Communist groupings was to strengthen its position against India. India itself declined to join in any alliance directed against the Soviet Union or Communist China, and tried to dissuade other Asian countries from doing so. But clashes with China over the disputed frontier in the Himalayas caused India to think better of an isolated neutrality and to seek support abroad, not however from other non-aligned countries – which were bound together by no mutual obligations of assistance – but from Britain, America and the Soviet Union, non-alignment now taking the form of getting help from both Washington and Moscow simultaneously against Peking. Pakistan countered this development by concluding an *entente* with China. The Indian Communist Party was split in two, one part claiming that China was right in its conflict with India and the other taking a national patriotic line and calling for defence of India's frontiers, even though it meant supporting a bourgeois government against a Communist state.

In the years immediately after the end of the Second World War the Soviet propaganda line was that Asian nationalist leaders such as Nehru, Aung San and Sukarno were not really striving for independence at all, but were disguised puppets of the British and Dutch imperialists; only the Communists could lead the colonial peoples to a real national independence. This was the period when local Communists in several Asian countries made bids for power through armed insurrection – in central India, in Burma, in Malaya, in Indonesia and in the Philippines. None of these revolts was successful; only in Vietnam, where the nationalist movement had come under Communist leadership already in 1945, and where for geographical reasons it was easy to obtain supplies from China after the Communists' victory there, was there a substantial and permanent extension of Communist power in South or South-East Asia. These disappointing results discouraged the Soviet Union, still led by Stalin up to 1953, from further attempts at promoting immediate Communist revolutions in the area, and the policy was abandoned in favour of diplomatic approaches to the new national governments, which had in any case demonstrated by their political actions that they were no mere puppets of the colonial powers, but entities with wills of their own. Even before Stalin's death Soviet policy was showing more interest in the governments of Third World countries than in their ineffective local Communists, and after the end of the Stalin era a rivalry carried on through diplomacy and economic aid to selected countries was more in keeping than incitements to armed revolt with the new slogan of 'victory through peaceful competition with capitalism'.

It was not for long, however, that the competition remained peaceful. Within the Third World there were national expansionist and irredentist ambitions which, although no longer directed against European colonial governments, continued to exploit the emotions of anti-imperialism and could be used by the Soviet Union to divert and weaken Western powers still involved in the areas concerned. Egypt under the leadership of Nasser hoped to unite the Arab world under its own hegemony by the destruction of the new state of Israel, which had successfully come into being in 1948 and was henceforth a thorn in the side of all Arabs. Because Britain had created a 'National Home for the Jews' in Palestine after the First World War, and because the U S had advocated a partition of Palestine after the Second, the existence of Israel was blamed on Western imperialism, and this attitude was a factor highly favourable to Soviet attempts to gain influence in the Arab world. The fact that in 1948 the Jews fought the Arabs with arms obtained from Czechoslovakia with the approval of the Soviet Union made very little impression on Arab minds; it had never indeed been widely known. At that time Egypt and the other Arab states had appeared to be under firm British ascendancy, and support for Zionism had seemed to Moscow to be the best way of upsetting the British apple-cart in the Middle East. But in the following years there was a radical change in Soviet policy; it was found that Jews in the Soviet Union had developed sentiments of attachment to Israel which were held to be incompatible with Soviet patriotism, and there was an officially sponsored revival of traditional Russian anti-semitism. Meanwhile Nasser with his anti-British Pan-Arab nationalism had come to power in Cairo. Soviet policy therefore became anti-Israel, and pro-Arab. It could not be claimed that any issue of ideological principle was involved, because, whatever had been the origins of the Jewish settlement in Palestine – and there had been a substantial community there even before 1914 – Israel was undoubtedly by 1955, when Russia began supplying arms to Egypt, a nation with its own territory, resolved to fight for its own independent existence. The contest was between nations, and could not be brought under the categories of a class struggle; it was indeed a supreme irony of the situation that a Communist Party was legal in Israel but not in Egypt. But in making itself the patron and sponsor of Pan-Arabism and its declared objective, the elimination of Israel, the Soviet Union certainly gained a great advantage in terms of international *Realpolitik*, for whereas Israel was a mere strip of territory between the Mediterranean and the Gulf of Aqaba, the Arab world stretched from Muscat to Morocco, comprising by 1967 thirteen states with votes in the United

Nations and including within its confines the richest oil-fields in the world. Since America and Britain were un-willing to connive at the extinction of Israel, they could never bid as high for Arab favour as the Russians, how-ever much they might try to exert influence in Arab countries.

In Indonesia the Soviet Union was able to acquire a similar influence by sponsoring an aggressive nationalist policy with an anti-Western edge to it. Sukarno had already in 1945 declared that Malaya must be a part of the new Indonesia, and this was a goal of which he never lost sight, though he recognized that time was needed for its attainment. In the meantime, after the formal recog-nition of Indonesian independence by Holland in 1949, Sukarno found a preliminary objective for the highly emotional militant nationalism which was his political speciality in the claim to Irian or western New Guinea, a land of very primitive people retained by the Dutch under their administration after the rest of the former Netherlands East Indies had been handed over to the new Indonesian state. Sukarno announced that Indonesia would liberate Irian by force and the Soviet Union con-signed weapons to the Indonesian army for the purpose; after a few airborne landings – in which the liberators were handicapped by the fact that the local inhabitants could not understand their language or why they had come – the Dutch yielded and Sukarno gained a great victory. No major Western power was prepared to assist the Dutch; they received only advice to come to terms with Indonesia. But when Sukarno, encouraged by his success in Irian, turned his attention to Malaya – or rather to Malaysia, the federal state formed when Britain relinquished sovereignty over its territories in northern Borneo – he had to contend both with the independent Malayan state and with Britain, which had guaranteed its defence. Sukarno hesitated to make outright war on Britain, but adopted a policy of 'confrontation' which included infiltration of armed bands across the land frontier in Borneo and airborne and seaborne raids on Malaya. The Soviet Union supported Sukarno with large supplies of arms and with diplomatic intervention at the United Nations, where the Soviet veto was used to prevent a condemnation of Indonesia as an aggressor by the Security Council. The Soviet Union thus gained preponderant influence in Djakarta, for the US, although not directly involved in the confrontation with Malaysia, could not take sides against its British ally, and no other Western power counted for anything in Indonesia.

As regards the prospects of Communism, the situation in Indonesia differed from that in the Arab world, for there was a powerful Communist Party in Indonesia which used Sukarno's 'guided democracy' and 'confrontation' to increase its strength. But this, instead of adding to the influence of the Soviet Union, brought about the ruin of the Soviet policy based on support for Indonesian nationalism. In the first place the Indonesian Communists, full of fervent militancy, rejected the line of the CPSU on international strategy as too moderate, and followed the more exciting revolutionary advice being preached from Peking. Further, and largely as a consequence of this, the socially conservative officers of the army, despite their goodwill towards the Soviet Union as supplier of their weaponry, became more and more anti-Communist in domestic affairs. Finally, after the attempted *coup d'état* of 30 September 1965 – in which a Communist conspiracy appears to have exploded prematurely – there was a ferocious mass repression of the Indonesian Communists, and the army used its Soviet equipment to crush the resistance of those who took to arms. The new military regime, then set up, abandoned confrontation and concentrated its efforts on rescuing Indonesia from the bankruptcy into which the country had been plunged by the financial profligacy of Sukarno; Indonesia swung back into the Western orbit, and the only consolation for Moscow was that the setback for Peking was even more complete.

In giving support to North Vietnam for its 'liberation' of South Vietnam the Soviet government did not of course risk the kind of outcome that happened in Indonesia, for the government of North Vietnam was already a Communist one and its army was fully controlled by the Party. But the backing of North Vietnam and its Viet Cong vanguard involved risks of a different kind, for South Vietnam was under the protection of the U S and it was hardly to be expected that the U S government would allow it to be overrun without a struggle. In supporting a specifically Communist offensive against a position held in effect by U S forces Moscow was challenging them in a way that it did not do in assisting attacks on Israel or Malaysia, and it was hardly in the spirit of peaceful coexistence. The reason appears to have been the need felt in Moscow not to leave the field of revolutionary leadership to Peking. Communist China was ready to back North Vietnam whether Russia did so or not and claim the credit for the victory if it were gained. To avert this outcome the Soviet Union committed itself to full moral and material support for North Vietnam and even established its reputation as a better friend to the cause than China, for it was able to provide various kinds of modern military equipment which China did not produce or lacked in sufficiency for its own forces. However, the fact that Soviet support for North Vietnam had an anti-Chinese edge to it did not make it the more acceptable to the U S, whose soldiers were being killed with Russian weapons, and as the scale of the war grew Soviet–U S relations were subjected to an increasing strain.

There was finally the arrival of Communist power in the western hemisphere with the establishment of the Castro regime in Cuba in 1959 and the extension of the concept of the Third World to include Latin America. Krushchev had to back down from his ill-advised attempt to install ballistic missiles in Cuba in 1962, and the U S reaction at that time showed that Washington would in future regard any similar Soviet move in or around the

Caribbean as a threat to its vital interests. But Cuba remained a Communist state and Castro did his best to use it as a base for stirring up revolutions in other countries of Latin America. The Latin American countries, linked with the US in a loose continental association, could not be regarded as non-aligned; however, their generally underdeveloped and semi-colonial economic character, relative poverty and political instability gave them a certain Third World character, and in Maoist propaganda Asia, Africa and Latin America were regularly bracketed together in contrast to the industrialized countries of North America and Europe. This idea received organizational form when the semi-official Communist front, the Afro-Asian Peoples' Solidarity Organization (AAPSO), was given a Latin American supplement at a conference in Havana in February 1966. There was evidence that on this and other occasions Soviet influence was exerted to restrain Castro from the more extreme provocations towards which his revolutionary romanticism and fanatical hatred of the 'Yanqui' were continually driving him, and the same influence was used with various Latin American Communist parties to dissuade them from responding to Castroite propaganda. The Russians were no doubt apprehensive of a situation in the western hemisphere which would compel them to choose between repudiating a Communist or quasi-Communist revolutionary upheaval and getting into a really dangerous collision course with the US. Up to the autumn of 1967 Castro's incitements had not produced serious trouble in other Latin American countries. But during that year events opened up a new and unexpected prospect of revolutionary warfare of which Castro seemed likely to take the fullest advantage. The Black Power movement suddenly emerging out of the liberal Civil Rights Campaign in the US was not in its origin Communist, nor did its crude racialism have any genuine Marxist context, but it was a movement which could very easily be brought into alignment with international

Communism, and parts of its propaganda, such as its condemnation of Israel in the Arab–Israeli war, showed that it had already acquired connexions abroad which were unlikely to diminish with the passage of time. The Black Power leader, Stokely Carmichael, after leaving the U S in August of 1967 went first to a conference in Havana, where he issued a kind of declaration of war against the U S with the support of Castro's Cuba, and then went on to visit North Vietnam, Algeria, Syria and Egypt, being received in all these countries as if he were already the head of a government. In this strange outburst of revolutionary violence, erupting not in mountains or jungles of near or remote lands, but in the heart of great U S cities – yet not proletarian in the old Marxist sense – there was the menace of a crisis which, if it were to become fully 'internationalized', could bring the world to war more fatally than any other issue of the time.

20. Fifty Years After

The year 1967 marks the fiftieth anniversary of the insurrection which gave power to the Communists in Russia. It is also the centenary of the publication in Hamburg of the first volume of Marx's *Das Kapital*.

In the Soviet Union, devoted to the principles of Marxism–Leninism, Lenin has long loomed bigger than Marx, and in China both Marx and Lenin have been eclipsed by Mao Tse-tung. Marx must still nevertheless be reckoned the founder of modern Communism, and it may be of interest to consider how he would see the world if he could revisit it in 1967. He would certainly be pleased to find that fourteen sovereign states had come to call themselves Communist and accepted him as a prophet. For one who had so little success in his lifetime this would be highly gratifying and would be firm evidence that he had been on the right track in his interpretation of the movement of history. There would certainly, however, be some things that he would find puzzling or disappointing. He would, first of all, be surprised to observe that, although the countries converted to his faith now numbered fourteen, several of them appeared to be in quite primitive stages of economic development, while the nations which he knew best and from which he had hoped the most – France, England and Germany – had rejected the Communist gospel, except for the eastern part of Germany, where, he would be informed – if he had an impartial source of information – that it had been imposed, not by an uprising of the German proletariat, but by an invading Russian army. He would discover also that the most industrially developed of all the capitalist nations – the United

States of America – seemed to have been the least affected by his teachings. He would find difficulty in understanding how it could be that the countries of advanced industrial development, in which, according to his doctrine, 'the centralization of the means of production and the socialization of labour reach a point where they prove incompatible with their capitalist husk', had not had proletarian revolutions, yet countries much less advanced had been consumed by the flames of Marx-inspired insurgency. He would be disturbed to learn that Mao Tse-tung had conquered China in the name of Marxism with an army of peasants, and that his principal lieutenant had declared that the coming world-revolution would be extended from the predominantly agrarian regions of the world to the more urbanized and industrialized areas. This for Marx, with his disdain for 'rural idiocy', would be a monstrous reversal of the proper order of things.

Looking at the capitalist world, he would have to admit that he had made errors in his forecasts of its development. He would see giant concentrations of capital, mergers and combines in plenty, yet there would still be far more competition and marketing contention than his theory allowed. He would hear of a great economic depression in the early 1930s which would be welcome confirmation of his views on the trade cycle, but also learn that since then capitalism seemed to have resorted to financial devices which greatly reduced the incidence of these disasters. He would still find great wealth and widespread poverty, but he would be perplexed at the failure of social history to produce that extreme polarization of rich and poor which he had anticipated. Above all he would be surprised – and perhaps more dismayed than pleased – to discover that the industrial working class was neither as poor nor as powerless as it should be. Standing in the workers' car park of an American factory he would be hard put to it to recognize a proletariat which should have been ground down in ever deepening poverty over the three quarters of a century since his death. He would indeed find poverty in that American city, but it would not be that of the regular industrial workers on whom Marx had counted to make socialist revolution; it would be that of a *Lumpenproletariat* recruited from former share-croppers and agricultural labourers drifting northward from the agrarian South and non-industrial Puerto Rico. And if he cast his eyes further afield he would find all over the underdeveloped regions of the world urban agglomerations full of surplus population from poverty-stricken rural areas – people who could hardly be called workers because they had never had any regular work since arrival in the cities, the underdeveloped countries having too little industry to employ them and the US an industry with too much machine handling and automation. Among these rootless masses there was certainly scope for revolutionary agitation – as Detroit discovered in the summer of 1967 – but it was not the proletariat as Marx had foreseen it.

Marx would find that the working-class movement in capitalist society had both realized and failed to realize his expectations. It had gained successes which had transformed the social landscape since the days of the great expansion of industrial capitalism in the early nineteenth century. By the bargaining power of its labour unions and by the political pressure of its voting strength in democratic elections it had brought about a sustained rise of working-class standards of living through higher wages, better conditions of work and governmental or municipal social services. But it had done all this without achieving socialism; the greater part of the economy was still carried on by private enterprise which provided the productive expansion required for higher living standards. It was no longer to be expected, therefore, as Marx had thought, that capitalism would be replaced by socialism because of the desperation of vast masses of utterly destitute workers who had 'nothing to lose but their chains'. If a socialist reconstruction of the economic order was to come about in advanced industrial countries (otherwise than through external coercion) it must be because a sufficient number of people were convinced that it would ensure both higher standards of living and a fuller human life for all citizens. The Marxist could no longer rely on an explosion automatically triggered by the contradictions of capitalism to hurl mankind into Utopia; the socialist ideal had to be advocated on its merits in order to make converts. Moreover, it had not been in the era since 1917 a matter of mere futurist speculation to discuss what a socialist society would be like; by 1967 there were a number of specimens which could be observed and studied for purposes of comparison. The debate had indeed long tended to be concerned less and less with Marxist theory and more and more with matters of fact: the conflict between the Communists' official versions of their achievements and analyses made by sceptical critics. Whether the Communists could win what Khrushchev called 'victory in peaceful competition with capitalism' depended largely on whether the more or the less favourable views of Communist practice came to be generally accepted in the West. There were wide differences of view even among the best qualified observers of conditions in Communist countries and no unanimous verdict in the controversy was to be expected. There was nevertheless a broad consensus on the main characteristics of Communist societies which was in general accordance with the accounts they gave of themselves. These characteristics could be compared not only with features of contemporary capitalist societies but also with the ideal of socialism as projected by Marx. We may be sure that if Marx were visiting the lands of Communist rule in the centenary year of the first appearance of *Das Kapital* he would not fail to notice any divergence of the social reality from what he had expected it to be.

Basically he would have been well pleased to see that

the Communists had not only seized power in a number of countries but had also made a collectively owned economy work to a degree which refuted the predictions of those economists who had predicted that such a system must soon collapse because of its inherent inefficiency. But he would be very surprised at the attention being given in the Soviet Union fifty years after the capture of power by the proletariat to questions of incentives, market indices and the profitability of enterprises. He would recognize the old language of capitalism and he would perceive also in the men who used it a striking family likeness to the Victorian 'captains of industry' who had been such commanding figures in his own time – brisk, efficient, hard-working, hard-faced men who had an ambition to 'better themselves' and acquired social status and moral respectability in the process of making money. It would be good to see that the new society had produced such competent economic leaders. But where was the victorious proletariat? Where were the horny-handed sons of toil who had wrested the power of the state away from the bourgeoisie in order to remake the world nearer to their hearts' desire? Marx would not find them among the swarming administrators, the bustling Party secretaries or the prosperous executives of business enterprises. He would find them if he went to look for them, but they would not be anywhere near the seats of power. If he were to read a book by a disenchanted Marxist, *The New Class* by Milovan Djilas – which he would not be able to buy in the Soviet Union – he would understand why they were not there. Theoretically they owned the means of production, but in practice the bureaucratic managerial class which controlled the operation of the economy were their employers and masters just as the bourgeoisie had once been. An intermittently benevolent Party-state might concern itself paternally with their welfare, but if they had any grievances their chances of redress were hardly greater than they had been before the rise of political democracy in the nineteenth century and much less than they were for their fellow-workers in contemporary bourgeois democracies, for, although they had their trade unions, these were strictly controlled from above by the Party, and although they had a democratic parliamentary franchise, they could only vote for persons nominated or endorsed by the Party.

It would indeed be the Communist Party itself which would be the greatest puzzle for Marx on his visit to the Soviet Union in 1967. He had never imagined anything like it. His League of Communists had been merely an instrument for making a revolution; it had been assumed that once the workers had captured the state power they would exercise it through freely elected bodies, from which indeed the bourgeoisie as the vanquished class would have to be excluded but from which nobody whom the workers might choose could be kept out. But now the 'vanguard of the proletariat' had transformed itself into a permanent authority over the whole people, possessing a monopoly of power and receiving an auto-matic endorsement from an electorate which had no alternative for which it could vote. The men who directed the Party had had their origin in the old pro-fessional revolutionaries of Lenin's time; they were still professionals, but not as revolutionaries. They were the masters, the rulers, the establishment. Revolution was now only for export to Vietnam.

Confronted with the Soviet regime as it existed fifty years after the proletarian revolution Marx would be hard put to it to discern any sign of that 'withering away of the state' which should have been its consequence. Even though it was no longer so oppressive and blood-thirsty as it had been in the time of Stalin, it was still a mighty coercive force, controlling the lives of its citizens to a far greater extent than did the states of bourgeois democracy and even exercising a censorious supervision over literature and the arts. Marx had believed that the state-power and its organs of repression should be kept in operation as long as the bourgeoisie continued to be a threat to the revolutionary proletariat, but could the bourgeoisie still be such a danger fifty years after Lenin had formed his Council of People's Commissars? Marx would no doubt be told that, even though there was no longer a serious risk of a bourgeois reaction in the Soviet Union and the whole people was, as everyone knew, solidly united behind the Soviet government, a strong state structure was still necessary because of the danger from foreign imperialists; Hitler had after all invaded and nearly overrun Russia and since his demise there had been even more dangerous warmongers lurking in Wall Street. Marx might be convinced by this argument, but he might also reply that if there was indeed such unanimous support for the regime, it would be better to allow a little more freedom to the people, who would then support it even more strongly.

Apart from the question of the need for an undiminished state power for political purposes, Marx would certainly be interested in what had happened to ordinary criminals under Communism. His belief had been that human beings were essentially good and socially minded in their conduct, but the system of private property with its craving for possessions and its competitive acquisitiveness had corrupted them. The same social order that produced conquering kings and barons, financial speculators and exploiting capitalists produced also thieves and bandits, who, unlike the others, were on the wrong side of the law. But the criminal and his kindred of beggars, drunkards, wastrels and hooligans were not so much the enemies as the victims of society; under the socialist order they would rapidly disappear, for everyone would have the opportunity to earn a living through honest work and nobody would be stimulated to theft or fraud by a code which encouraged all men to seek personal gain and self-enrichment. If reality had been in accord with this theory, the Soviet Union by 1967 should have been relatively free from ordinary crime, and if there was still a residue of hardened criminals from the bad old days, the younger generation, which had been brought up in Soviet schools and had never known capitalism, should display to the full the virtues of a race of human beings from whom personal self-interest and the profit motive had been eliminated. Yet juvenile delinquency had become as much of a problem in Russia as in the countries of the bourgeois West, with the difference that whereas in Russia the official view went on claiming that such things as adolescent thieving and hooliganism were survivals of bourgeois mentality, nobody in the West thought of attributing the increase of indictable offences by teen-agers to the persisting influence of their grandfathers.

From his survey of the Communist scene in 1967 Marx might thus well have come to the conclusion that history had repeated in a somewhat different form that frustration of the high hopes of an immediate millennial transformation which it had brought about after 1850.

We have seen how he expected quick results from the revolutionary upheaval forecast in the *Communist Manifesto*, how the course of events disappointed him, and how he – and even more Engels – came more and more to seek social change within the boundaries of the new emerging bourgeois democracy rather than through 'the violent overthrow of the whole existing social order'. Nearly three decades after his death the dream of the *Communist Manifesto* came true; political power was captured by a proletarian revolution in one of the principal countries of the world, landlords and capitalists were expropriated and a socialist economic order was created. Yet in the years that followed events took a course quite different from the direction in which by Marxist theory the revolution pointed. There was no victorious counter-revolution, no restoration of private capitalism. But instead of workers' control there was the dictatorship of a single party increasingly identified with an administrative bureaucracy; instead of an economic levelling, a differentiation of incomes comparable to that of the bourgeois world, and instead of progress towards liberty and the 'withering away of the state' the growth of a mighty, authoritarian governmental power suppressing not only all political opposition but every kind of ideological dissent.

Confronted with such an outcome of his revolutionary gospel, it is likely that Marx would again conclude, as after 1850, that more time was needed, that his New Jerusalem was further away than he had supposed and that some more democratic way forward must be found. He might even hope that with the new Communist experiments in market economics on the one hand and the economic interventions of the state in capitalist countries on the other, the two social systems might gradually approach nearer to each other, exerting a mutual influence in a long period of close contact in a spatially contracted world. But any such optimistic vision of the future must reckon with the vested interests of the ruling Communist parties. They are ultimately what Communism signifies today and these great engines of despotic power have hardly anything to do with Marx and very little to do even with Lenin.

Select Bibliography

Probably the best account in English of Marxism as a system of political thought is GEORGE LICHTHEIM'S *Marxism: A Historical and Critical Study*, published in 1965. A good biography of Marx by an admirer is FRANZ MEHRING'S *Karl Marx*, which first appeared in an English translation in 1938; there is also a biography from a more detached point of view by Isaiah Berlin published in 1948. A critical comparative study of Marxism and Leninism is provided by JOHN PLAMENATZ in his *German Marxism and Russian Communism*; the Russian intellectual background to the reception of Marxism in the late nineteenth century is described by S. V. UTECHIN in *Russian Political Thought* and by S. R. TOMPKINS in *The Russian Intelligentsia*. DONALD TREADGOLD in *Lenin and His Rivals* has given a good account of Lenin's contests for leadership in Russian revolutionary politics, and S. V. UTECHIN in an annotated edition of Lenin's *What is to be done?* explains the significance of this key text. There is a very large literature on Lenin, but there are very few works which combine an adequate account of Lenin's life with a satisfactory political history of the revolution which he made; outstanding is LOUIS FISCHER'S *The Life of Lenin*, which appeared in 1964.

The most complete historical account of the party founded by Lenin is LEONARD SCHAPIRO'S *The Communist Party of the Soviet Union*, which carries the story to the death of Stalin, with an epilogue 'Since Stalin Died'. The treatment is detached and critical; more favourable to the regime are the successively produced volumes of E. H. CARR'S *A History of the Soviet Union*. W. H. CHAMBERLIN'S *The Russian Revolution*, published 1935, is still a standard work for the Bolshevik seizure of power and the civil war in Russia; much additional information is contained in DAVID FOOTMAN'S *Civil War in Russia* which came out in 1965. The original *élan* of the revolution is perhaps best conveyed in JOHN REED'S *Ten Days that Shook the World.*

There is still no adequate biography of Stalin and the production of one will continue to be a task of very great difficulty because of the extraordinary suppression or falsification of records which prevailed during the period of his rule. In the words of Ivan Maisky, the former Soviet Ambassador in London: 'One of the consequences of the cult of personality of Stalin is the great shortage of memoirs by Soviet politicians, diplomats and leaders of the party, the state and the army, and without a sufficient amount of such materials the historians of the future will find it difficult to understand the events connected with the birth and development of the USSR.' ISAAC DEUTSCHER has written an excellent biography of Trotsky, based on the 'Trotsky archives', which were preserved by the latter in exile, but his attempt to write a life of Stalin failed to get close to the subject because of the insufficiency of the evidence. For Stalin's early life SOUVARIN'S *Stalin* is still a good authority, but Stalin the despot becomes less and less open to observation as the story proceeds and the mystery that surrounds him invests his deeds with an almost supernatural quality of horror. ROBERT PAYNE'S biography also suffers from this trend and falls back on guesswork for much of the dictatorial phase of Stalin's career. The recent publication of the memoirs of his daughter Svetlana, now living in exile in America, gives a convincing portrayal of Stalin as a family man, but she was not in a position to know much of her father's political life. For our knowledge of a man of such hidden and devious ways attention must be given to the accounts of defectors from the Soviet secret services, notably WALTER KRIVITSKY'S *I Was Stalin's Agent* and ALEXANDER ORLOV'S *The Secret History of Stalin's Crimes*, despite the necessarily biased and sensational character of such material. Contemporary appraisals of the Soviet regime during Stalin's lifetime vary enormously in their estimates of its achievements; SIDNEY and BEATRICE WEBB'S book *Soviet Communism: a New Civilization?*, which became the Bible of 'fellow-travellers' during the thirties, may be taken as representative of the glorification of the regime by its admirers, while N. DE BASILY'S *Russia under Soviet Rule* stands in contrast as a formidable indictment of it. A special class of literature on Stalin's Russia is provided by memoirs of foreigners who began as enthusiastic admirers of the Soviet system, but became progressively disillusioned until they emerged as unsparing critics of it; mention may be made of EUGENE LYONS, *Assignment in Utopia*, and FREDA UTLEY, *The Dream we Lost*; more unfortunate in her personal fate than either of these was ELINOR LIPPER, whose book *Eleven Years in Soviet Prison Camps* gives a terrible picture of *le monde concentrationnaire* created by Stalin's dictatorship. In the case of PAUL WINTERTON, who was *News Chronicle* correspondent in Russia during the thirties, it is possible to compare literary products of both the devoted and disillusioned phases; *Russia with Open Eyes* is a fervent eulogy of Stalin's rule at the height of the Great Purge, while *Inquest on an Ally*, written after the Second World War, is a bitter attack on Soviet policies.

The denunciation of Stalin by Khrushchev in his secret speech to the Twentieth Congress of the CPSU is analysed by BERTRAM WOLFE with comments on a translated text in *Khrushchev and Stalin's Ghost*. There is a good biography of Khrushchev by MARK FRANKLAND (Penguin, 1966), written after his fall from power, and an earlier and less favourable study of his career by GEORGE PALOCZI-HORVATH under the title of *Khrushchev's Rise to Power*. A collection of Khrushchev's speeches and writings was published in Moscow in English during his tenure of high office under the title of *For Victory in Peaceful Competition with Capitalism*.

For the history of the Communist International FRANZ BORKENAU'S *European Communism* and *The Communist International* (1938) are classic works. For later development of the international Communist movement HUGH SETON-WATSON'S *The Pattern of Communist Revolts* (1953) and *Neither War nor Peace* (1960) are important studies.

For Chinese Communism MAURICE MEISNER'S *Li Ta-chao and the Origins of Chinese Marxism* is an extremely important work, as it explains the peculiar development which Communism underwent in China from the time of its first introduction. *A Documentary History of Chinese Communism*, edited by BENJAMIN SCHWARZ, CONRAD BRANDT and JOHN FAIRBANK, is of great value for the study of the Communist Party's past policies. For the political career of Mao Tse-tung there is a biography by STUART SCHRAM (Penguin, 1966), who has also made available a number of relevant documents in *The Political Thought of Mao Tse-tung*. The hitherto obscure period of Mao's career between 1927 and 1935 has recently been illuminated by two important works, JOHN RUE'S *Mao Tse-tung in Opposition* (1966) and SHANTI SWARUP'S *A Study of the Chinese Communist Movement* (1966). For the attempts of the CPSU to guide the revolution in China in the early days two studies are outstanding: ROBERT NORTH'S *Moscow and Chinese Communists* and CONRAD BRANDT'S *Stalin's Failure in China*. For the more recent 'dispute' between Moscow and Peking there is DONALD ZAGORIA'S *The Sino-Soviet Conflict 1956–1961*, and R. S. ELEGANT'S book *The Centre of the World*, which discusses the convergence of the Chinese claim to leadership of the world Communist movement with traditional Chinese ethnocentrism. A revealing collection of documents on Communist China's brief experiment in free criticism appeared in 1960 under the title of *The Hundred Flowers* edited by RODERICK MAC-FARQUHAR. *China in the Year 2001* by HAN SUYIN (New Thinker's Library; Penguin) is a stimulating view of the current history of China seen through Chinese eyes. A symposium on contemporary China under the title of *The Chinese Model*, edited by WERNER KLATT (1956), discusses the Chinese Communists' claim that their revolution provides the exemplar to be followed by all underdeveloped countries.

For the study of Communist publicity *Communist Propaganda Techniques* by J. C. CLEWS is a most valuable contribution; another significant work is F. C. BARGHOORN, *The Soviet Cultural Offensive*.

In July 1967 *Survey* brought out a special number entitled *The Soviet Revolution 1917–1967: A Balance Sheet* to review the developments of Communism since Lenin's time and current trends in Soviet society.

Index

More about Penguins and Pelicans

Penguinews, which appears every month, contains details of all the new books issued by Penguins as they are published. From time to time it is supplemented by *Penguins in Print*, which is a complete list of all books published by Penguins which are in print. (There are well over three thousand of these.)

A specimen copy of *Penguinews* will be sent to you free on request, and you can become a subscriber for the price of the postage. For a year's issues (including the complete lists) please send 30p if you live in the United Kingdom, or 60p if you live elsewhere. Just write to Dept EP, Penguin Books Ltd, Harmondsworth, Middlesex, enclosing a cheque or postal order, and your name will be added to the mailing list.

Another Pelican book is described overleaf.

Note: *Penguinews* and *Penguins in Print* are not available in the U.S.A. or Canada

The Communist Manifesto

Karl Marx and Friedrich Engels
with an Introduction by A. J. P. Taylor

The complete text of the political tract which has
exercised so great an influence on the world in the
past century.

In a special introduction to this new edition
A. J. P. Taylor charts the progress of the *Manifesto*
from persecuted obscurity to global reverence and
examines the relevance of Marx's nineteenth-century
ideas to the realities of modern politics.